GROWing WITH CARE

Using Greenery, Gardens and Nature with Aging and Special Populations

by Betsy Kreidler

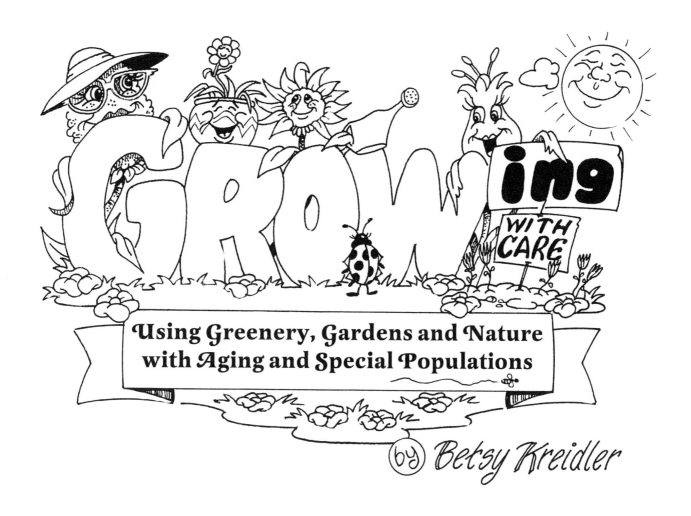

GROWing
WITH CARE

Using Greenery, Gardens and Nature with Aging and Special Populations

by *Betsy Kreidler*

Venture Publishing, Inc. • State College, Pennsylvania

The author and publisher caution the professional to be sensitive to the abilities and limitations of the participants. Professional judgment and research on your part is required.

Production Manager: Richard Yocum
Manuscript Editing: Michele L. Barbin
Illustrations: Mark D. Smith

Library of Congress Catalogue Card Number 2002107290
ISBN 1-892132-34-6

Dedication

To my mother-in-law, Helen Kreidler, who lost her memory to Alzheimer's disease, but never forgot her love of flowers.

Table of Contents

The Gardening Calendar

References and Resources

Appendix of Fill-in Forms ... 137

Index 141

List of Tables and Figures

Foreword

The miracle of living things is that they grow. The greatest joy of a human life is often found in helping things grow. We are gardeners by nature. In fact, the very idea of tending a garden is a useful counterweight to our sometimes frenzied modern lives. Too often these days we seek answers in the rush of technology. The faster we go, the fancier our gadgets become, and the more we need the pleasures that gardening affords.

People need to have contact with living things, and older people need that contact more than most of us. Older people have often found it difficult to maintain their connection to the soil. Our challenge is finding clever and creative ways of helping older people re-form that precious bond. This book teaches us how to take the garden to our elders no matter what their abilities may be. It shows us how to create a team that can, along with seeds, soil and water, make magic happen.

Go ahead, plant the seed, take the chance, help a garden grow—and you will help people grow. That is the essence of our society's commitment to our elders. They deserve more than just food and water, medicines and therapies. Like all living creatures, our elders deserve a chance to grow.

Dr. William Thomas
Founder of The Eden Alternative™

Preface

This book is for staff, residents, volunteers, and people of all abilities who participate in the daily routines of tending to indoor plants and outdoor gardens. In my suggestions for greening up, many options are provided for developing individual plans and styles, and for the maintenance of greenery and gardens in all stages of growth. I hope that both amateur and experienced green thumbs reading this guide will think of it as a comfortable tool to be used for the care and nurturing of people and plants.

My approach to bringing plants and people together is modeled after a transforming way of caring known as The Eden Alternative.™ In his foreword, Dr. William Thomas, founder of The Eden Alternative, discusses the need of older people "to have contact with living things." In fact, the Eden Alternative concept brings together residents, children, companion animals, plants, and gardens on a daily basis in the environment known as the *Human Habitat*. Residents that have been gardeners all their lives, or those who have only a passing interest in gardening, are enriched by the vibrant, growing atmosphere.

The methods suggested here are adaptable to any residential care home or day community desiring to introduce greenery and gardens to its residents or clients. This book divides the gardening information into four phases: Prepare to Grow, The Indoor Gardens, Outdoor Gardening, and the Gardening Calendar. Each phase takes the readers step-by-step through the preparation, organization, and "digging in" aspects that contribute to the growth of houseplants, flowers, vegetables, herbs, a variety of wildlife, and ultimately, the residents.

Although getting to the palm tree in the sunroom or soil in the flowerbeds may seem to involve a lot of gardening talk rather than action, please have patience. Building a sense of ownership, self-confidence, and trust within the indoor and outdoor gardening teams is essential for establishing a healthy crop rather than a weedy disappointment.

Growing with Care is primarily a guide for encouraging people to enjoy life through gardening. The approaches suggested here all not all-inclusive. For instance, you won't find a section on "feeding roses" or "raising pumpkins." For that reason, I encourage mentoring by knowledgeable volunteers such as Master Gardeners or experienced community members. Building a library of in-house gardening books will also contribute to the gardeners' knowledge and increase spontaneous activities as well.

This book is designed to be read and shared by a group. The planning and organizing of the gardens are best approached through a team effort. The cultivation of group energy and shared resources is encouraged throughout each phase and step of the gardening journey. Sharing in-house and community resources greatly reduces the time and attention needed to plan, develop, and implement a gardening environment. When those first cuttings sprout roots and that last pumpkin is carved, however, the fruits of many labors can be celebrated together.

My heartfelt gratitude to the following people who contributed in numerous ways to making this book possible: Jack Lizotte; The American Horticultural Therapy Association; John and Marge Schott; the residents of Winebrenner Village; the Hancock County Master Gardener Program; Paul Kreidler; Dr. Bill Thomas; Geoffrey Godbey; the staff of many Eden Alternative homes; and Michele L. Barbin.

My very best wishes to all people who garden from their hearts.

—Betsy Kreidler

Phase I
Prepare to Grow

Much of this book is based upon the philosophical ideals of The Eden Alternative.™ The Eden Alternative encourages careful planning in an open and comfortable atmosphere that offers various opportunities for residents to care for greenery, companion animals, and wildlife. This book focuses mostly on indoor and outdoor gardening aspects of The Eden Alternative with tips for attracting wildlife and increasing enjoyment of companion animals within the Human Habitat. The mission statement of The Eden Alternative reads:

> The core concept of The Eden Alternative is strikingly simple. We must teach ourselves to see the [nursing home] environments as habitats for human beings rather than facilities for the frail and elderly. We must learn what Mother Nature has to teach us about the creation of vibrant, vigorous habitats.

The greenery, gardens, and natural aspects of this environment, or Human Habitat, do not stand alone as a program or isolated activity. Rather, they are a part of the everyday experience of people living and working in an Eden Alternative home.

The concept of The Eden Alternative is based on the following ten principles:

1. The Three Plagues of loneliness, helplessness, and boredom account for the bulk of suffering in a human community.

2. Life in a truly human community revolves around close and continuing contact with children, plants, and animals. These ancient relationships provide young and old alike with a pathway to life worth living.

3. Loving companionship is the antidote to loneliness. In a human community, we must provide easy access to human and animal companionship.

4. To give care to another makes us stronger. To receive care gracefully is a pleasure and an art. A healthy human community promotes both of these virtues in its daily life, seeking always to balance one with the other.

5. Trust in each other allows us the pleasure of answering the needs of the moment. When we fill our lives with variety and spontaneity, we honor the world and our place in it.

6. Meaning is the food and water that nourishes the human spirit. It strengthens us. The counterfeits of meaning tempt us with hollow promises. In the end, they always leave us empty and alone.

7. Medical treatment should be the servant of genuine human caring, never its master.

8. In a human community, the wisdom of the elders grows in direct proportion to the honor and respect accorded to them.

9. Human growth must never be separated from human life.

10. Wise leadership is the lifeblood of any struggle against the Three Plagues. For it, there can be no substitute. (*Eden Alternative Journal*, 2002)

Since The Eden Alternative is highly integrated within this book, the following description of terms and ideas will help the reader understand the structure of the gardening process as it takes place in Eden Alternative nursing and assisted living homes. Keep in mind that these are guidelines, not rules. Each home directs its own journey into The Eden Alternative—the basic philosophy remains, but details can differ.

Activity Staff: These people are part of the Home's resident activities department and may or may not be on the Plant Care Team. They assist the residents to interact with the indoor and outdoor gardens. They also may be volunteers under the supervision of the activities personnel.

Community: The interacting, interdependent population within a nursing home, assisted living, or other residential care home. These people include the residents, all staff, resident companion animals, family, friends, child day care or school children, and volunteers. This may also refer to citizens at-large who live in the town or city near the nursing home, but will be specified as such.

Human Habitat: A truly human community where life revolves around close and continuing contact with children, plants, and animals. In this environment human relationships are strengthened, human–animal bonds are fostered, and opportunities are created to give meaningful care to other living creatures.

Management: Usually refers to the Administrator and other paid staff that have taken the Eden Alternative Associate training, and are coordinating the initial educational process for beginning The Eden Alternative concept in a residential care home.

Mentor(s): A local person or people available to coach/teach the Plant Care Team in the identification and care of the plants. Depending on the availability and particular expertise of mentors, there may be one or several who interact with the Plant Care Team.

Neighborhood: The physical designation of the nursing home's various resident living arrangements, formally known as *wings* or *units*. Rather than medically oriented names such as the "North Wing," or "3rd West," neighborhoods have pleasant, homey names such as "Mulberry" or "Rosewood."

Neighborhood Team: The designated staff caring for residents, either directly such as certified nurses' aides or nurses, or indirectly such as housekeeping personnel. These staff members work in neighborhoods and are considered a team. The residents are a major part of this team, and, as with each team member, have a voice in the overall operation of the neighborhood. Staff such as social services, housekeeping supervisors, administration, and dietary personnel not having a designated resident living area are assigned to neighborhood teams.

Neighborhood Committee: Designated members of the neighborhood team who research and bring information back to the team for specific decisions. Some examples may be a change of interior decoration; adopting a cat or dog; acquiring new indoor plants; or constructing outdoor gardens adjacent to that neighborhood. One of these committee representatives may attend the plant committee meetings or might be an actual member of the plant committee.

Plant Committee: The informational and educational guidance team behind the planning, creation, and care of indoor and outdoor gardens. The team consists of paid staff, residents, volunteers, and appropriate community-at-large members, all who have an interest in the benefits of gardening. Basic indoor and outdoor gardening information is compiled by the committee for use by the individual neighborhoods.

Plant Committee Chairperson: This is generally a paid staff member. He or she may be from any department or personnel level. The major requirement is an interest and belief in the benefits to the residents of indoor and outdoor gardening and nature. This chairperson has either volunteered or willingly accepted this position. This person conveys suggestions about plant and garden placement, construction, and plant care to the individual neighborhood teams.

Plant Care Team: This refers to the people caring for the indoor and/or outdoor plants. The Team may include staff members, residents, and volunteers. A staff member is usually the supervisor and scheduler; a volunteer such as a Master Gardener may be the mentor or a staff or family member may take that responsibility. Quite often the activities personnel accept this duty and integrate plant care with resident activities. The individual neighborhoods may choose to care for their own plants with consultation by the mentor.

Purple-thumbed: A lighthearted reference to people who believe in the positive benefits of gardening and nature but are inexperienced in the functional aspects of growing and caring for plants and gardens.

A great deal of the so-called groundwork is laid out in these committees long before any real soil is turned. The basic concepts are discussed, volunteers are involved, and tentative plans are made and remade around the table and on paper. This vital planning phase will help all participants develop a sense of ownership and active involvement within the gardening environment. All productive planning begins with a basic evaluation. Opinions and feedback from all residents, staff, volunteers and visitors is, of course, most welcome.

How Green Are We?

In many homes, staff and residents have started a garden or have cared for houseplants long before the introduction of The Eden Alternative. As you begin the journey, and a plant committee or similar planning team is formed, the committee chairperson can personally examine the indoor plant and outdoor garden situation to form an understanding of what is already in place. The committee can then build on these earlier efforts, revise what has been

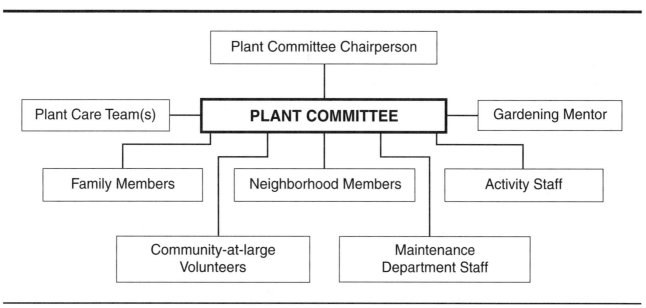

Figure 1   Sample Flow Chart for the Plant Committee

done, or, in some cases, start over. If the evaluation is conducted after The Eden Alternative has been adopted, members can still benefit from the information and insight discovered through an evaluation.

Each existing indoor and outdoor garden space should be identified and evaluated separately. This information is then brought to the plant committee or neighborhood for discussion. The information is a starting point only, and does not need to be detailed. Discuss the following with emphasis placed on the indoor plants as the first priority. This general overview will give the plant committee perspective as it begins the indoor greening process.

The following are question guidelines to consider:

For Indoor Plants

- Where, in relation to each unit, are the indoor plants located?
- Who cares for the plants? When is care given? Is time for plant care allowed within the staff members' work shift?
- Can the residents easily reach the plants to care for them?
- Are tools available for plant care? Can the tools be adapted for participants with motor skills difficulties?
- How is water obtained?
- Is plant care included in daily resident activities?
- Is plant care training offered to residents, staff, and volunteers?
- Is there information readily available about toxic and nontoxic plants?
- Is a procedure in place in the event of plant poisioning?
- Are on-site houseplant how-to books available for participants, especially staff? (See *References and resources*, p. 133 for suggested titles.)
- Are volunteers and/or community resources involved or available?

- Is there a budget for plants, tools, and materials?

Outdoor Gardens

- Is a resident garden in place? Where, in relation to the building, is it located?
- Is the garden plot accessible to both residents who are ambulatory and in wheelchairs?
- Can the residents operate the exit door?
- What equipment and tools are available?
- How is water obtained?
- Who on staff now cares for the garden? Is separate time allowed within the employee's shift to care for the garden?
- Is gardening included in the residents' scheduled activities?
- Have staff members been trained in gardening techniques?
- Are gardening books on hand for staff?
- Is information available pertaining to toxic plants?
- Are volunteers involved? Are other community resources used?
- Is there a budget available?

Forming Policies for Plant Care

Prior to attracting Plant Care Team members, flexible policies, guidelines, and procedures can be formed by the Plant Committee in relation to the following:

- indoor plant care training for staff
- supervision of the Plant Care Team(s)
- the number of Team members needed
- staff time involved
- volunteer advisor/mentor
- continuing education
- plant maintenance and monitoring
- evaluating resident involvement
- the use of nonharmful plants, or creating an approved plant list

- an emphasis on practicing organic gardening methods
- an emphasis on safety including first aid for plant ingestion or allergic reactions to plants that may effect residents, visitors, and animals

Having answers to these issues before asking staff to commit time to plant care will demonstrate consideration of all employees' concerns, and will provide the Chairperson with a frame of reference. As various concerns and situations are discussed, the original policies may need to be altered for practical purposes.

Attracting Employees to Join the Plant Committee

Each Home will follow its own path for committee formation based on The Eden Alternative guidelines. The plant committee chairperson may be the activities director or coordinator, a dietary employee with a long-standing houseplant hobby, or a physical therapy assistant who has seen the value of garden therapy. As with all relationships in The Eden Alternative, the two operating guidelines are:

1. As management does unto staff, so shall staff do unto Elders.
2. All decisions belong with the Elders or as close to the Elders as possible. (Thomas, 1998)

Employees do not have to sprout green thumbs to join the plant committee. It is likely, however, that several staff members have houseplant collections in their homes, and are competent plant caregivers. Employees who have had their own outdoor gardens are even easier to find.

The tricky part may be convincing these valuable people to lend their talents to the committee. What will it take to attract volunteers from the staff who may already feel overloaded? Some suggestions:

- Include lots of positive spontaneous *and* planned talk about committee membership and opportunities to participate and grow as a person and employee.

- Make and distribute colorful, upbeat posters to each department. Ask for "purple-thumbed, plant and flower-loving people." List the benefits of joining.
- Arrange for community resources to train staff in indoor and outdoor plant care, such as Master Gardeners, greenhouse representatives, or garden club members.
- Assure staff that plant care personnel will have training and continuing education opportunities.
- Arrange media coverage of plant team training, award certificates, certifications, and hold other events. Recognize and identify these vital volunteers with a lapel pin and/or appropriately lettered apron or t-shirt for the Plant Care Team.
- Be sure to address employees' time devoted to the construction of needed items such as cold frames, raised beds, garden paths, and other resident-oriented gardening structures. Will this time be compensated?
- How will materials be obtained? Donations are welcomed, but will maintenance have to pick up the donations on their own time?
- Are there any other appropriate esteem-building statements or offers?

Community Resources and the Plant Committee

Every community contains specialists in various fields of indoor and outdoor plant identification, care and propagation, and related use of materials, tools, and equipment. For example, a plant expert from the community can offer knowledge and experience to assist in the selection, placement, and care of indoor plants. In another example, if raised planter boxes or plant carts are needed, representatives from supply stores are valuable resources.

As contacts for committee members are made, the plant chairperson can describe the committee's needs and give a brief overview of The Eden Alternative as directed by management. An orientation tea or evening reception may encourage reluctant volunteers to show up for the "no obligation" introduction. Most community groups and individuals will be very interested, but may need to attend an actual meeting before agreeing to a long-term commitment. The following resources are usually available in every community and may be contacted by phone or in person:

- **Family members and friends** who visit frequently

- **Master Gardeners:** These people have completed a variety of plant and gardening classes, and have fulfilled community volunteer requirements or are looking for more hours. Call your County Cooperative Extension Office.

- **Garden and herb clubs, organic garden clubs:** Talk with the club presidents who will have the master list of all members in the organization.

- **Florists, greenhouses, nurseries, herb shops** usually have degreed or trained personnel on staff. Ask specifically for a person well-acquainted with indoor plant care, vegetable and herb gardening, or other areas of interest to the plant committee.

- **Wholesale garden and greenhouse suppliers** have vast equipment knowledge.

- **College or university staff** in horticultural or botany programs may not be able to sit on a committee due to academic commitments, but can be excellent sources of information. Often they have their own greenhouse and may offer observation opportunities, on-site visits, and cuttings.

- **Schools** (especially vocational) may have a gardening, landscaping, or greenhouse program, information, and offer opportunities for on-site discussions.

- **Hospitals and rehabilitation centers** with garden therapy programs may have an in-house horticultural therapist.

- **Botanical gardens** have a wealth of information, ideas for activities, informed personnel, and reference books.

- **City and county parks** often employ a horticulturist.

- **Zoos** usually have a plant expert and greenhouse.

- **Senior centers** have participants with years of experience caring for houseplants and gardens.

- **Interior design and maintenance companies** in larger cities specialize in indoor plant care for large companies and may be willing to share some indoor landscaping tips.

- **Large indoor malls** may have their own plant care specialists who will share their experience.

- Managers of **lumberyards, hardware stores, and home supply centers** may be willing to donate supplies if they are included in part of the planning process.

Through interaction with community citizens, organizations, commercial enterprises, and the family members and friends of residents, the Home will gain knowledge, and the opportunity to obtain materials, volunteers, training, and a network of lifetime connections and support.

How the Principles of The Eden Alternative™ Relate to Plants and Gardens

Now that the existing indoor and outdoor garden situations are better understood, it's time to review how The Eden Alternative principles relate specifically to residents and gardening. Understanding how these principles relate to the gardening process will give staff the confidence to use nature in new and creative ways, and to become specialists in their areas of contribution.

Keep in mind that the main purposes of the greenery are to encourage the residents to feel at home, and provide a natural, comfortable atmosphere for everyone who lives in, works at, or visits the home. It is intended to be an enjoyable experience where on-the-job learning, trial and error, and celebration of successes, both small and large, are of equal importance.

Principle 1:

The Three Plagues of loneliness, helplessness, and boredom account for the bulk of suffering in a typical long-term care facility.

Plants and gardens provide many opportunities to relieve this kind of suffering. Sharing gardening experiences can revive precious memories of times spent in family gardens.

Many residents may choose to watch others work with the plants, but will benefit from the fellowship and mental stimulation. Some will want to get their hands in the dirt and will enjoy being productive. The major benefit will come from knowing they are part of a group with a common cause and interest. On the other hand, a resident who chooses to work alone can experience satisfaction and a sense of accomplishment as well.

With a little practice, staff will find many opportunities to bring love into bloom. Looking around the sunroom or taking a resident for a garden walk will produce a topic to share. Sprouting seeds, new leaves and flowers, a pocketful of acorns, or ripened cherry tomatoes are just a few examples.

Although a stroke had left Madeline without the use of her right side, her mind was as sharp as ever. She found an outlet for her love of growing flowers and vegetables by attending garden club meetings and would ask for houseplant starters for her window. She played an active part in planning the garden crops and shared her recipe for bread-and-butter pickles with lip smacking results for residents and staff.

Principle 2:

Life in a truly human community revolves around close and continued contact with children, plants and animals. These ancient relationships provide young and old alike with a pathway to a life worth living.

In this new environment, plants and people grow in response to each other. The institutional setting gives way to a sense of home where life grows and changes as the residents are encouraged to participate in caring for the plants and animals to the best of their ability.

The changing seasons in the garden help keep the residents oriented mentally while they start seeds, plant seedlings in the garden beds, tend to maturing plants, and harvest flowers or vegetables. Lifelong skills such as using a watering can and snapping green beans are opportunities for success. Accessible plants and raised garden beds motivate residents to plant, weed, and harvest on their own.

Moving to a nursing home is never an easy change for anyone. The choice of the best medical care, cleanest building, and most compassionate staff cannot duplicate the resident's home environment. In the Human Habitat, indoor plants and outdoor gardens contribute continuity to a portion of the resident's life which otherwise would be left behind. A new resident's impression of being placed into a life-ending institution is changed for the better, as he or she becomes aware of the lively surroundings.

The location of plants and gardens is very important. Are there barriers keeping people from the plants? How will the residents water plants on their own? Can the residents open the outside door to get to the garden? Do residents need assistance to care for their personal plants?

Remember that when residents were in their own homes, houseplants were in a favorite bay window or on a kitchen table. The kitchen faucet was always handy for water and the watering can was kept within easy reach.

The residents of Mulberry Lane loved to watch seeds sprout on the table by the sunroom window, but often chairs or tables would hinder their ability to get close enough to see the sprouts. The staff and residents discussed this problem at their team meeting, and solved this furniture placement problem together.

Principle 4

To give care to another makes us stronger. To receive care gracefully is a pleasure and an art. A healthy human community promotes both of these virtues in its daily life, seeking always to balance one with the other.

The opportunity to give care and to accept responsibility for other living things gives residents a continued sense of being needed and capable. Staff will most likely take the lead to encourage residents to care for personal plants. A member of the Plant Care Team can meet with residents to discuss personal preferences for plants, and any special needs the residents have in relation to plant care.

Taking care of plants is a cooperative activity where the shared experience is the reward—not necessarily well-groomed plants. When the Plant Care Team members maintain the houseplants or gardens, they should invite a resident to join them, either in the actual gardening or in observation of the plants. The gardener-to-gardener companionship, the aroma of the soil, and the warmth of the sun can often provide as much therapy as any standard medical intervention.

Interaction with children in an indoor plant room or outdoor garden is a world of experience unto itself. Residents and children assist each other to learn, grow, and enjoy the use of the natural setting. Children enjoy the thrill of discovering a sprouted cucumber seed, and the residents can explain various ways to train the cucumber vines to climb a trellis. The residents share stories about their childhood—Victory gardens planted during World War II, or how canned and preserved produce would feed them for a year. Some of the children listening to these stories have never seen vegetables outside of a supermarket display.

Living plants are nurtured in this child–adult partnership, but the most important result of gardening together is the growing relationships between the children and residents. This bond produces mutual pride and a sense of accomplishment in having successfully raised crops to eat, display, and share with friends and family.

Residents in a Home that employed local community service workers were very involved in planning their garden. Their sense of ownership was obvious. One day the residents became upset by the apparently well-meaning actions of one of the community workers. He had meticulously separated the hills of sprouted squash seeds that the residents had planted, and carefully replanted them in neat rows. The residents insisted that the Activities Coordinator help them replant the seeds in their original hills. The squash sprouts survived and did well.

Principle 5

Trust in each other allows us the pleasure of answering the needs of the moment. When we fill our lives with variety and spontaneity, we honor the world and our place in it.

Variety is at the staff's fingertips as the staff and residents plan what kinds of flowers and vegetables to plant from seed. By placing the seed-starting shelf where residents can observe it daily, each sprouting seed can be an event to celebrate.

The variety of texture, fragrance, color, size, and shape in the plant world is vast. Tools and accessories are topics for discussion, and catalog browsing is pure entertainment.

Plant and garden materials are ideal for a variety of on-the-spot staff and resident interactions, most of which are simple and require little preparation. The feel of a cuddly lamb's ear leaf, the fragrance of a rose or the spicy scent of a sprig of lemon thyme, and the thrill of pulling a rosy radish or crispy carrot take only a minute to accomplish. These little acts of companionship leave both residents and staff members with a lasting sense of satisfaction.

One morning as a staff member watered the flowerbed, she discovered a small beetle with what appeared to be a pure golden shell. She carefully brought it inside to show to everyone. Much to her surprise, it faded to a dull ladybug color indoors. Was it a trick of the light? Disappointing maybe, but definitely a spontaneously shared discovery.

Who Will Care for the Indoor Plants and Outdoor Gardens?

Employees voluntarily fill these positions. The Plant Care Team may be in the activities department or housekeeping; they could be certified nurses aids, or dietary staff members. Each unit may have its own Plant Care Team or a single Plant Care Team might take charge of the entire Home's plant population—indoors and out. In some cases, outside professional help is contracted to care for the plants in the larger public areas, or an individual is hired to coordinate the habitat care.

"How can I get my day-to-day work done *and* do the plant care?" will be one of the first questions asked by staff before they agree to care for the plants. This is where your plant care guidelines will provide a basis for employees to agree to the task.

Training in plant care, supervision, number of team members with backups for illness and vacations, the time involved, scheduling of plant care, a professional advisor/mentor, and continuing education must be made clear prior to beginning the plant program. Outdoor garden care teams also can briefly be discussed at this time. The outdoor garden team may be different from the indoor team, or may be composed of the same people.

Lots of encouragement and some amount of persuasion may be needed for the staff members to commit to caring for the greenery. The presence of the gardening mentor as a member of the committee will be very reassuring as will the promise of continued support from management and the plant committee chairperson.

Offer Training and Education about Plant and Garden Care

There are a variety of ways in which training and continuing education may be obtained. Time involved, expense, transportation, and specific benefits for people directly responsible for the plants, and the resulting benefits for the Human Habitat, must be considered. The plant committee can discuss the following possibilities:

- The Master Gardener program, through the local County Cooperative Extension Service offers, for a fee, a forty-hour course covering a wide range of indoor and outdoor topics. This course might be appropriate for a member of the Plant Care Team to attend.

- A Master Gardener mentor may be available to supply on-site training and support free of charge. This may involve several mentors, each specializing in a different area.

- Botanical gardens or horticultural associations may offer seminars (for a fee) with a variety of houseplant and garden information.

- Garden clubs of various types may supply volunteers for on-site training in houseplant or garden care.

- City and county parks' programs offer workshops on wildlife topics.

- Tips, ideas, and methods may be shared by vocational schools, colleges, and other facilities having garden programs.

Start Indoors, then Move Outside

One of the purposes of the Human Habitat is to bring nature to the residents as much as possible. This can be done with less effort, and at almost any time of the year, with indoor plants and activities. Establish your indoor greenery to reach the most people first. It may even encourage more involvement when plans for the outdoor gardens are being discussed.

Chances are, most Homes have already developed an outdoor garden prior to beginning an indoor one. People are generally more knowledgeable about vegetable and flower gardening than indoor plants. It is less stressful, however, if the outdoor garden is simplified or reduced until the staff and residents are acquainted with the indoor plants and their needs.

After the indoor plants are introduced, the Plant Care Teams have mapped out a routine, and the resident garden clubs have been formed, the staff can then devote time to outdoor garden planning.

Involving Residents in the Green and Growing Habitat

Involve the residents as early as possible in the greening up process. In order for the residents to feel a sense of ownership and participation, their opinions and preferences *must* be considered before major changes in their living areas or personal spaces are planned.

After introducing the concepts of The Eden Alternative to residents and families, the specifics of the indoor greenery can be discussed. The reasons for, and benefits of, the plants can be the topic of a morning coffee klatch. Try *How indoor plants take care of people* (p. 13). During this gathering, staff can encourage reminiscing about houseplant hobbies, ask about favorite flowering plants, what their mothers or fathers taught them about plants, and so forth. Suggestions can be taken from the residents at this time for placement of plants in the nursing home, preferred types of plants, how to meet light requirements, helping care for residents' plants, the formation of the Plant Care Team, and other planning elements. A brief discussion about poisonous plants can be held at this time. This will lay the groundwork for resident interest and involvement in decision making.

Children, Residents, and Plants

Youth–elder interactions can be among the most rewarding experiences for everyone involved. Success occurs with thoughtful, regular planning in cooperation with the child daycare staff, school-teachers, and other youth group leaders.

Many facilities have already started intergenerational relationships and have routines in place. As with any involvement between elders and children, it is helpful to follow certain guidelines for communication, planning, safety, discipline, and appropriate age-related activities.

Joint discussion and planning time between the nursing home's plant activities staff and community-at-large youth leaders is essential.

Homes are not expected to know all the techniques needed to interact with children. The Home's responsibility lies in planning the plant activities, having materials ready, and understanding the abilities of the residents in attendance. Preparation sessions with teachers or youth leaders will help to adjust the activities as needed to fit the age level and needs of the children. At the same time, the Home's staff can explain the needs and abilities of their residents to the teacher. For resources about intergenerational gardening activities, please see *References and resources* (p. 133).

Animals, Birds, and Plants

Greenery can be beneficial, but occasionally harmful to companion animals. Before asking for house-plant donations and before purchasing any specific plants, reliable references about toxic and nontoxic indoor and outdoor plants should be obtained for both people and pets. A good reference for plants that are potentially harmful to pets is available from the ASPCA National Animal Poison Control Center. Named *Household Plant Reference*, it may be obtained for a nominal fee by contacting:

> ASPCA
> National Animal Poison Control Center
> 1717 South Philo Road, Suite #36
> Urbana, IL 61802
> Phone: 217–337–5030; Fax: 217–337–0599

Several books describing natural, holistic approaches to pet care discuss beneficial plants, and ways to prevent animals from eating harmful plants. These include:

Frazier, A. with Eckroati, N. (1990). *The new natural cat: A complete guide for finicky owners*. New York, NY: E. P. Dutton.

McGinnis, T. (1996). *The well cat book: The classic comprehensive handbook of cat care*. New York, NY: Random House.

Stein, D. (1993). *Natural healing for dogs and cats*. Freedom, CA: Crossing Press.

Brainstorming for the Future

The plant committee can go wild in this area with ideas and dreams for the perfect indoor and outdoor habitat. Wouldn't it be great to have a resident-friendly greenhouse attached to the dining room? Would you like to have the convenience of an indoor, portable raised flower/plant box for each floor? How about a weatherproof, vine-covered garden seating area for residents? Would automatic doors to the garden be more convenient for everyone? Imagine sturdy, low-maintenance raised beds; pathways for wheelchairs; fountains, outdoor wildlife shrubs, light carts, and so on. Write down all these ideas to present to your community resources and grant organizations, and review them periodically. Ask the Plant Care Teams and activities staff to take notes during their plant care sessions and activities. What else would be nice to have?

Phase II
The Indoor Gardens

Part 1: Beginning to Grow

Congratulations! Your Home is about to begin a growing adventure with people and plants. It may seem overwhelming right now; but in time, the plants and their needs will become almost as familiar as the faces, personalities, and needs of the residents. The staff on the Plant Care Team will be seen in a new light—be prepared for popularity and a lot of positive attention.

This next section is directed toward the Plant Care Team and will help them to get down to the nitty-gritty of organizing the indoor plant selection, care schedule, and choosing personal plants with residents.

Some encouraging words for management and the Plant Care Team as they get ready for indoor and outdoor gardening:

- Educate the indoor and outdoor Plant Care Teams.

- Communicate with residents, staff, and local community.

- Start with easy plants and crops.

- Remember that resident involvement takes many forms.

- Success comes with mutual enjoyment—not perfect plants.

How Indoor Plants Take Care of People: Some Basic Facts

Plants are amazing, living beings which produce helpful substances for people and other creatures that live nearby. Oxygen and moisture emitted by plants refreshes and humidifies the air around the greenery. Plants have the ability to remove harmful air pollution, and some release chemicals that actually help to control and reduce molds and bacteria.

Prior to modern scientific studies people believed that plants and flowers placed in the room of an ill person would deplete the oxygen in the surrounding air. As a result, they placed plants out in the hallway at night. Fortunately, we now know that oxygen is emitted by plants. The natural process of photosynthesis (the conversion of carbon dioxide and water to carbohydrates and oxygen in the presence of light and chlorophyll) actually produces tons of oxygen each year and releases it into the air we breathe.

In studies conducted by the National Aeronautics and Space Administration (NASA) for more than 25 years, scientists were searching for ways to purify air inside planned moon bases. Working closely with renowned environmental scientist, B. C. Wolverton, NASA proved that houseplants can clean and refresh air in enclosed areas. This has become especially important as people spend more and more time indoors in "air-conditioned" buildings. Most of us are aware of the hazards of outdoor air pollution from auto and factory emissions, but what about the quality of our indoor air? Indoor air quality suffers equally. Ordinary items such as carpeting, cleaning products, draperies, paints, photocopiers, and ceiling tiles release potentially harmful chemicals into the air of homes and offices. Even people emit some chemicals that can be unpleasant in closed-in areas, such as a small chapel or dining room.

All residential buildings contain numerous materials and items known to release toxic vapors. One of the most commonly released toxic gases is formaldehyde. This gas is found in garbage bags, paper towels, tissues, fabrics, carpet backing, permanent-press clothing, plywood, and paneling. Other examples of common toxic chemical emissions are: cleaning products that release ammonia; floor coverings, paints, stains and varnishes that release formaldehyde, xylene, toluene, and benzene; photocopiers that release xylene, toluene and trichloroethylene; cosmetics, perfumes, colognes and nail polish remover that release alcohols and acetone vapors; and even people emit a combination of several of the above toxic gases.

Wolverton's research resulted in vital knowledge which supports the positive effects of individual plants on the quality of indoor air and the beneficial relationship between plants and people. In his book, *How to Grow Fresh Air*, he rates 50 houseplants according to their ability to remove chemicals from the air, the ease of growth, care needs of the plant, their resistance to insects, and the rate at which the plant releases moisture into the surrounding area.

Some plants that are well-suited to improve air quality, safe to handle, ideal for resident activities, and easy to maintain include:

- Areca palm (*Chrysalidocarpus lutescens*): This plant is one of the best choices for removing all tested air toxins found indoors, and releases large amounts of moisture into the air. It is considered potentially toxic to companion animals, however.

- Lady palm (*Rhapis excelsa*): Removes formaldehyde and ammonia; good moisture release.

- Bamboo palm (*Chamaedorea seifrizii*): Removes benzene, trichloroethylene and formaldehyde; releases moisture.

- Ficus tree (*Ficus macleilandii* "Alii"): Removes formaldehyde, xylene and toluene. Considered potentially toxic to animals, and may cause dermatitis with some people.

- Begonia (*Begonia semperflorens*): Effective in releasing moisture; fair at removing a variety of chemical gases.

- Prayer plant (*Maranta leuconeura*): Effective in releasing moisture; fair at removing chemical gases.

- Oakleaf ivy (*Cissus rhombifolia*): Good at releasing moisture; fair at removing chemical gases.

- Spider plant (*Chlorophytum comosum*): Removes formaldehyde; fair at releasing moisture.

Another important benefit of indoor plants is their ability to suppress mold spores and bacteria found in the air. Plants do this through the manufacture and release of substances called *phytochemicals*.

Keep these benefits in mind when choosing plants and then combine this knowledge with the awareness of plants that can be harmful to humans or animals. For further details on choosing plants to improve indoor air quality, read the book *How to Grow Fresh Air* (Wolverton, 1997).

Organizing Routine Plant Care

Before official plant maintenance begins, the Plant Care Team must decide who will care for which plants each week. Assuming that each unit has selected its Plant Care Team, or that there is one Plant Care Team who will care for all the indoor plants, and that the Team(s) have received adequate training, these questions can then be asked:

- Which day of the week is best for plant care? This can vary by a day, but should be as consistent as possible.

- Does the time of day matter?
- How much time can comfortably be allowed for plant maintenance?
- Will an interested resident volunteer be assisting the plant care person?
- Is there an orientation for plant care resident volunteers?
- Will the Team rotate plant care persons, or will the same Team work continuously?
- How will staff members' days off, vacation days, and illness be handled?
- Does the plant care need to be divided into certain locations for certain days? (More than one day may be needed to care for a large number of plants.)
- Who will make out the plant care schedule, and where will it be posted?
- How will this information be communicated and to which supervisors?
- How will the Plant Care Team member sign off from his or her regular job to begin the plant care?
- Who will be monitoring the plant care?
- Does the Team have special name badges, aprons, or t-shirts?
- Is the plant cart stocked and ready to go? Who restocks the plant cart?

Tools and Supplies for Indoor Plant Care

Appropriate tools for the job will make plant maintenance a pleasant and rewarding activity. Most of these items can be donated through community groups or by the Home's personnel and families. Gather up all available tools and equipment, and compare them with the following list of items the Plant Team will need:

- ❏ A notebook with a list of the plants, their location, plant care plans, attached pen
- ❏ The plant cart
- ❏ A safe storage place for the cart and means of locking up any chemicals
- ❏ An appropriate and easily accessible water source
- ❏ An appropriate utility sink for pot and tool washing
- ❏ A plastic caddie or shoe box for small items
- ❏ A large bucket with comfortable handle, labeled "for plant watering *only*"
- ❏ A large bulb syringe for collecting water from saucers under pots that are too heavy to lift
- ❏ A small bucket for collecting standing water
- ❏ One medium-sized watering can
- ❏ A sharp pointed, indelible marker or wax pencil (for plant labels and writing renewal dates on ends of florescent light tubes)
- ❏ Name labels for plants: may be galvanized, two-pronged stakes with horizontal plate on which to write common and scientific name, or plastic "sign" type with space to write. Plastic strip labels made with a label gun and attached to a galvanized plate last longer than ink.
- ❏ Scissors and/or branch trimmers (for ficus trees and large floor plants)
- ❏ Gloves (washable cotton, disposable latex, and vinyl)
- ❏ Houseplant fertilizer (water soluble or time-release pellets) in a moistureproof container or resealable plastic bag
- ❏ Sterile soil mix in a container with a lid
- ❏ A trowel or hand cultivator (digger)
- ❏ A feather duster
- ❏ A large plastic spray bottle
- ❏ Fels Naptha, castile soap, Ivory dish soap, or insecticidal soap concentrate for insect spray solution
- ❏ Trash bags (both large and small) for collecting dead leaves, trimmings, and paper trash
- ❏ Rags for mopping up water and soil spills
- ❏ A dust pan and brush

Other Items to Consider

- ❏ Moisture meters for large pots

❏ Cotton swabs or cotton balls (for applying rubbing alcohol to mealy bug casings) and a bottle of rubbing alcohol

❏ Two absorbent sponges for cleaning large plant leaves

❏ A hand-held vacuum (e.g., a Dustbuster) for cleaning up dry soil spills

Circulate flyers to staff and families to ask for tools and equipment. Make personal contact with garden clubs and give short presentations to individual clubs or leaders about the Home's indoor and outdoor gardening plans and its need for supplies and equipment. Commercial stores may also be contacted for donations.

The Plant Cart: Find It, Build It, or Buy It?

Set aside a cart specifically for Plant Care Team use. This assures that tools and equipment are easy to locate, maintain, and are portable. A permanent storage spot for the cart should be located in an accessible place yet away from major traffic patterns. Consider locating the cart near the water source and/or utility sink for easy clean up. Don't forget to lock up potentially harmful supplies or materials such as sharp tools, soap spray, fertilizer, insecticides, and rubbing alcohol.

Almost every nursing home has an extra aluminum cart, which can be outfitted with equipment for plant care. The compact style with three shelves works well, but any comfortable design will do as long as it can hold all the necessary items. Imagination and the maintenance department or a community volunteer can help make a personalized model too. Start with what's available at the home, become accustomed to routinely used tools and how they're carried, and design a custombuilt cart based on experience and personal knowledge. Civic groups will be more willing to contribute funds for a cart if a plan is in place.

Commercially produced carts are available at garden centers and through catalogs. A plant maintenance cart can be an excellent purchase for a garden or civic club to sponsor.

Take a Good Look at Existing Indoor Plants, Pots, and Locations

The Eden Alternative suggests that Homes first start greening up with *indoor* plants since this provides the easiest access to plants for all residents and provides the most health benefits from the plants filtering the air. Neighborhood resident representatives are encouraged to participate with the Plant Care Team as they examine the existing plants in a constructive manner. This examination will evaluate and record how the plants look now. This will help the Plant Care Team members to become more aware of the condition of the plants, decide how to improve the plants' overall health, and where to best locate each plant for the both residents' and the plant's benefit.

Working with the Plants on Hand

Before considering the ways and means of having plants donated or purchased, the Plant Care Team and resident representatives need to examine the plants on hand. The following steps can be taken to get started; some questions to answer prior to actual plant maintenance include:

• Do any of the plants have personal value to residents? *Don't discard any plant before searching for its owner.*

• Is the plant healthy and worth keeping? If it is heavily infested or rotting, suggest treating it to see the results, or consider discarding it.

• What is the common and scientific name of each plant? Identify each plant by its common and scientific names *and label it.*

• Is there is a reasonable risk of resident harm from plants identified as toxic or potentially toxic? Can these plants be moved to an area away from residents and animals to reduce the risk? Can some of these toxic plants be hung out of resident and animal reach?

After the existing plants are appropriately located and the Plant Care Team has discussed scheduling plant care, then the fun of selecting and getting more plants will begin. *Don't get ahead of the game.* Be sure to have the care schedule for existing plants worked out first.

Examining the Existing Plants and Their Environment

The Plant Care Team and its resident representatives will want to conduct this more detailed investigation by using the following inspection suggestions. Look at the type of pot in which the plant lives. Notice the containers: lift out pots placed inside larger pots, and examine hanging baskets inside and out as follows.

Do you see:

- The plant placed directly in a pot with the soil up to the top, or is the plant in a pot that was then set into a larger, more decorative pot?
- Is the soil evenly colored? or is there bark mulch or another special covering over the soil?
- Is the drainage saucer or bottom of the outside, decorative pot dry?
- Are the pots clean? (inside and out if two pots are being used)
- Are the leaves shiny, clean, and green?
- Are the leaves of fairly equal size and color, except for the new leaves at the tips of the stems?
- Is the plant evenly shaped with leaves growing equally all around the pot?
- Where is the plant located in relation to a light source? Is there a window within three feet of the plant, a traditional fluorescent ceiling light, or specialty grow light directly above the plant? Common light bulbs do not provide the kind of light plants need to grow. Is sunlight obstructed by a curtain, awning or tree?
- Are plants grouped together with sufficient "breathing space" between pots?
- Are hooks to hang pots placed firmly in the ceiling or wall with sturdy ropes and chains attached?

- Are the plants arranged so that a resident in a wheelchair can reach them? (Plant Care Team members might want to sit in a wheelchair and try to reach the plants.)
- Are there safety issues such as water on the floor, or pots and branches obstructing traffic?
- Is there evidence of confused residents using the larger pots as toilets? (Give the soil the sniff test.)

Now that the indoor plant situation is more familiar, the Plant Care Team and its resident representatives will want to discuss future plans with the plant committee and/or the neighborhood residents. These questions can then be considered:

- Has a Plant Care Team been formed for the neighborhood in question?
- What sort of plant care training has been offered?
- Has a scheduled time been arranged for plant care?
- Are the residents taking part in the planning process?
- Are more plants needed or wanted in the near future?
- Is more light needed to increase the plant population? Remember that plants need light from a window or artificial light (i.e., traditional fluorescent or "grow" light) placed directly above them; recessed lighting is not enough. (See *Indoor plants and lighting*, pp. 34–37.)
- Does the neighborhood have, or want to have, a sitting area where the residents are surrounded by plants? Discuss seating for visitors in these areas.
- Are the plants accessible to the residents for spontaneous care (e.g., watering and dead leaf removal) and for observation of growth and change (e.g., new flower buds forming, an invasion of spider mites)?
- Is there a work area set up for transplanting, activities with children, and other planned social and spontaneous plant activities?

Safety Concerns for People and Pets

The safety of residents in a nursing home is an issue that is heavily emphasized for many good reasons. This is especially important when working with residents involved with indoor gardening activities. Even though the activity may be designed for fun and positive feelings, staff must take all precautions to prevent harm to the residents, visitors, companion animals, or themselves. Common sense and planning will contribute greatly to success.

At the same time, staff must weigh the benefits with costs of taking potential risks to allow the residents freedom of choice. If in doubt about the safety of an activity or plant, discuss it with the Plant Care Team, neighborhood residents, or, if the risk is immediate, the neighborhood's supervisor. Keep the following in mind as the plant activities are being planned, and while the activities are carried out:

Environment/Work Area

- Allow adequate floor space for walkers and wheelchairs.
- Prune large branches or leaves that hang in aisles.
- Wipe up water and soil spills immediately; use "wet floor" signs as needed.
- Keep all tools off floors and seats.
- Keep track of all tools being used.
- Paint tool handles bright yellow with black bands or dots to make them easier to see.
- Keep tools oiled and free from rust.
- Use appropriate tools for the job (e.g., a trowel rather than a wooden spoon to mix soil).
- Hang pots on firmly anchored hooks; check hanging wire and ropes for security; check height for head clearance.
- Use nontoxic plants. Only use "potentially toxic" plants with common sense after discussing it with the neighborhood supervisor and caregivers. Know which toxic plants to avoid altogether.
- If, as a last resort, it is necessary to use commercial insecticides, use only the sprays or dusts recommended for the identified insect or disease. Read the label thoroughly. Follow all recommended user precautions. Keep residents, pets, and visitors away from the area during use. Immediately store sprays and dusts out of reach in a locked storage cabinet as soon as the job is completed.
- Fasten lids securely on fertilizers; store out of reach in a locked cabinet immediately after use.

Resident and Other Individual Concerns

- Always consider the ability of the resident when giving him or her a garden tool.
- Consider adapting tool handles for comfort (e.g., wrapping handles with nonslip material or encasing them in foam cylinders).
- Consider using weighted or therapeutically angled tools (consult an occupational therapist).
- Create a comfortable workstation for potting up, arranging flowers, taking cuttings, and other garden-related activities.
- Provide adequate lighting for resident and staff activities.
- Provide latex, vinyl, and garden gloves as needed.
- Be aware that perlite, vermiculite, and peat moss particles can get into eyes. Moistening these materials prior to use will reduce this risk. Use a potting soil mix rather than individual ingredients.
- Understand that a resident's allergies may play a part in reluctance or refusal to participate in the hands-on aspect of gardening. Discuss concerns with these residents, their families, the nurse in charge, and, if needed, the resident's doctor.
- Consider the perception of some residents when planning to use large plant containers

that sit on the floor. Will the pots look like toilets?

- When planning to serve food or refreshments, check residents' dietary charts and allergies with the nurse in charge. Also check children's food and plant allergies with their teacher, parent, or guardian prior to using herbs in foods or teas during intergenerational activities.

- Check with the nurse in charge (and schoolteachers) prior to using untried hand lotion, fragrances, soaps, or creams on residents (or children).

- *Know emergency response to injury and toxic plant ingestion.*

Knowing Which Toxic Plants to Avoid

The intent of this next section is to give the Plant Care Team reasonable guidelines for keeping and placing indoor plants currently on the premises, and for choosing new plants to add to the Home. A number of the plants that were already in place may be considered *toxic*, *potentially toxic* (usually for companion animals), or even *lethal* by the sources noted at the end of this section. Table 1 (pp. 20–22) is a compilation of lists from various parts of the United States and Canada— it is *not* all-inclusive. It will, however, help you get started, but more research on your behalf will help you develop the plant toxicity list most appropriate for your area.

Toxic plant lists vary somewhat in content from source to source; poison control boards and university horticultural departments may differ with each other and with the ASPCA's *Household Plant Reference*. Different geographical regions emphasize local poisonous plants. Common sense and a reliable houseplant advisor are your best guides.

The Plant Care Team should always have *toxic plant information* from the previously mentioned sources on hand. Keep in mind that even nontoxic plants can become a hazard if they have been sprayed with toxic pesticides, or if pesticides have been added to their soil. This is often the case with plants bought at greenhouses or through a wholesale company. Know where your plants come from, and what chemicals have been used on them.

The neighborhood team may decide to keep, relocate, or discard certain plants based on the plant committee's evaluation. These decisions may be assisted by the following considerations:

- Residents' state of mind, and the possibility of their eating plants

- Presence of cats and dogs, and their tendency to eat plants

- Presence of children and the possibility they might eat plants

- Symptoms described by the Poison Control Board and ASPCA information

- Accountability and liability issues

- Relocation options for toxic or questionable plants

If there are otherwise healthy plants which appear on the toxic list yet have been in the Home for some time, they can be moved to an appropriate area where there is minimal chance of resident or animal contact. Healthy and attractive, but questionable, smaller plants can be hung out of reach, placed in offices, or in nonresident, animal-free areas.

It's easier to start enriching the indoor garden environment with nontoxic plants than it is to remove donated or purchased plants which might be harmful. Before any requests are made for indoor plants, or choices are made about purchasing additional plants, the Home's existing indoor plants should be identified and clearly labeled with the common and, if possible, scientific names.

Labels should be durable and have sufficient space to hold both names. Galvanized, two-pronged labels have space to write the names with indelible marker which can then be coated with clear nail polish to keep the ink from rubbing off. Plastic labels from a label maker are more durable and can be used in place of a marker. The staff will need an authority on houseplants to identify some plants accurately. Have two or three comprehensive houseplant books for reference as well. A Master Gardener or professional horticulturist volunteer can be asked to assist with identification.

Table 1   Some Toxic Indoor Plants

The plants in this list are considered toxic to people unless otherwise noted. Cut flowers arriving from a florist or a home garden also may be a risk. See *Some Outdoor Toxic Plants* (pp. 64–67) for a list of some common flowers used for cutting.

COMMON NAME	SCIENTIFIC NAME	TOXICITY NOTES
Air plant, Mother of millions	Kalanchoe pinnata	Potentially harmful to people; toxic to animals
Aloe, Burn plant	Aloe vera	Toxic to animals
Amaryllis	Hippeastrum puniceum	Minor concern for people; toxic to animals
Angel's trumpet	Brugmansia, Datura	**Can be fatal to people** toxic to animals
Anthurium	Anthurium varieties	
Apple seeds, Apricot pits (stems and leaves especially when wilting)	Malus, Prunus	**Can be fatal to both people and animals**
Areca palm, Butterfly palm	Chrysalidocarpus lutescens	Potentially harmful to animals
Arrowhed vine	Syngonium podophyllum	
Asparagus fern (berries)	Sprengeri, Densiflorus	
Avocado	Persea americana	
Azalea (florist and other varieties)	Rhododendron	**Can be fatal to both people and animals**
Begonia (some species)	Begonia	
Bird of paradise	Caesalpinia gilliesii	
Black cherry (pits, wilting leaves)	Prunus	**Can be fatal to both people and animals**
Blue gum (may be in dried arrangements)	Eucalyptus varieties	
Brunfelsia (Lady of the night; Yesterday, today and tomorrow)	Brunfelsia americana; B. australis	Toxic to people and animals
Buddhist pine	Podocarpus macrophylla	
Bunchberry	Lantana	
Burn plant	Aloe vera	Toxic to animals
Caladium (all varieties)	Caladium	
Calla lily	Zantedeschia aethiopia	Minor toxicity for both people and animals
Cannabis (marijuana, hemp)	Cannabis	Toxic to people and animals
Carnation	Dianthus caryophyllus	
Carolina yellow jessamine	Gelsemium sempervirens	**Can be fatal to both people and animals**
Chenille plant, Copperleaf, Three-seeded Mercury	Acalypha varieties	
Cherry (pits, wilting leaves)	Prunus varieties	**Can be fatal to both people and animals**
Chinese evergreen (all varieties)	Aglaonema varieties	Toxic to people and animals
Chives/onion family plants	Allium schoenoprasum	Toxic to animals especially cats
Christmas or Easter cactus	Schlumbergera, Zygocactus	Potentially harmful to animals
Chrysanthemum	Chrysanthemum varieties	
Cineraria	Senecio varieties	

Table 1　　Some Toxic Indoor Plants (continued)

COMMON NAME	SCIENTIFIC NAME	TOXICITY NOTES
Clivia	Clivia varieties	
Coleus (all varieties)	Coleus	Potentially harmful to animals
Croton	Codiaeum variegatum	Potentially harmful to animals
Crown of thorns	Euphorbia varieties	
Cyclamen	Cyclamen varieties	Toxic to people and animals
Daffodil, bulb (all varieties)	Narcissus	
Daisy, Mum	Chrysanthemum varieties	Potentially harmful to animals
Devil's ivy, Pothos	Epipremnum aureum	Toxic to people and animals
Dracaena (all varieties):		
Corn plant	Dracaena 'Massangeana'	
Dragon tree	D. 'Marginata'	
	D. deremensis 'Janet Craig'	
	D. deremensis 'Warneckei'	
Dumb cane (several varieties)	Dieffenbachia	Toxic to people and animals
Easter lily	Lilium longiflorum	Minor toxicity for people; all parts of plant may cause acute kidney failure in cats.
English ivy	Hedera helix	Toxic to people and animals
Eucalyptus (several varieties)	Eucalyptus	
Frangipani, Temple tree (all varieties)	Plumeria varieties	
Fig: Fiddle leaf, Rubber plant, Weeping, and others	Ficus lyrata, F. elastica, F. benjamina	
Fishtail palm	Caryota varieties	
Flamingo flower	Anthurium	
Glory lily	Gloriosa	**Can be fatal to both people and animals**
Grevillea	Grevillea varieties	
Hibiscus (tropical variety)	Hibiscus rosa-sinensis	Potentially toxic to animals
Holly	Ilex	Minor toxicity in people; toxic to animals
Hyacinth	Hyacinthus orientalis	Toxic to people and animals
Hydrangea	Hydrangea	Potentially harmful to both people and animals
Ivy, English	Hedera varieties	
Ivy, Grape	Ciccus rhombifolia	
Jade plant	Crassula argentea	
Jequirity bean, Crabseye, Precatory bean, Indian licorice (seeds; bright red with black eye; used in jewelry)	Abrus precatorius	**Can be fatal to both people and animals**
Jerusalem cherry	Solanum pseudocapsicum	**Can be fatal to people**
Jessamine, Carolina; Night-scented jessamine; Lady of the night	Cestrum	**Can be fatal to people**
Jonquil (bulb; all varieties)	Narcissus	

Table 1   Some Toxic Indoor Plants (continued)

COMMON NAME	SCIENTIFIC NAME	TOXICITY NOTES
Kafir lily	Clivia miniata	
Kalanchoe (all varieties)	Kalanchoe	
Lily (some types)	Lilium	Toxic to people and animals
Mistletoe, American and European	Phoradendron, Viscum album	
Moon flower (seeds)	Ipomoea alba	**Can be fatal to both people and animals**
Morning Glory (seeds)	Ipomoea violacea	**Can be fatal to both people and animals**
Moses-in-the-cradle	Rhoeo spathacea	
Mother-in-Law's Tongue (all varieties)	Sansevieria	
Narcissus (bulb; all varieties)	Narcissus	
Nectarine (pits, wilting leaves)	Prunus	**Can be fatal to both people and animals**
Norfolk Island pine	Auraucaria heterophylla	Potentially harmful to animals
Oleander	Nerium oleander	**Can be fatal to both people and animals**
Paper flower (thorns)	Bouganvillea varieties	
Peace lily (all varieties)	Spathiphyllum	
Peach, Pear pits	Prunus, Pyrus varieties	**Can be fatal to people**
Philodendron (all varieties)	Philodendron	Toxic to people and animals
Pittosporum (all varieties)	Pittosporum	
Plum (pits, wilting leaves)	Prunus	**Can be fatal to both people and animals**
Potato (sprouts, green skin)	Solanum tuberosum	Toxic to people and animals
Primrose (all varieties)	Primula	
Rattail crassula	Crassula lycopodioides	Potentially harmful to animals
Rubber tree	Ficus elastica	
Sago palm	Cycad	
Schefflera, Umbrella tree	Brassaia actinophylla	
Silk oak	Grevillea varieties	
Snake plant (all varieties)	Sansevieria	
String of beads	Senecio rowleyanus	
Sweet pea (seeds)	Lathyra odoratus	
Swiss cheese plant, Split-leaf philodendron	Monstera deliciosa	
Tulip (bulb; all varieties)	Tulipa	Minor toxicity for both people and animals
Umbrella Plant (indoor and bog plant)	Cyperus alternifolius	
Wandering Jew (green, purple, and varigated; all varieties)	Tradescantia, including but not limited to T. albiflora, T. fluminensis, T. zebrina	Potentially harmful to animals

Compiled from ASPCA, 1998; Burrows & Tyrl, 2001; Canadian Poisonous Plants Information System, 2002; Greater Cleveland Poison Control Center, 2002; Halpin, 1980; House Rabbit Society, 1994; Jones, 2001; King, 2002; Niering & Olmstead, 1979; University of California at Davis, 2002.

Any toxic plants discovered at this time can be relocated to places with light exposure and temperatures similar to where they were found.

When the time is right to request donations of new houseplants, a list of plants preferred by the residents and approved by the plant committee may be posted or distributed. As the plants arrive, they can be evaluated by the Plant Care Team and the houseplant advisor, and placed appropriately around the home. A coordinated response to well-meaning people who unintentionally try to donate toxic plants should be in place. Good public relations are a definite advantage.

The list of plants in Table 1 are considered *toxic to people and/or animals* and are commonly seen as *indoor* decorative plants, and gift plants. *This is only a partial list.* The decision for keeping these plants or allowing them to be brought into the home should be seriously reconsidered. Do *not* let the scientific/botanical names intimidate you. You don't need to remember them or even know how to pronounce them. They are simply for double checking if there is confusion about a plant's identity. For more complete listings, see the references mentioned on page 136, and contact your local poison control center, county extension agent, and/or university resources.

Some more common indoor decorative and gift plants considered *potentially toxic to animals and/or people* are included in this list. These are plants which don't usually cause a problem, but have shown enough evidence of symptoms when eaten to raise suspicion and warrant caution for animal owners and caregivers. Cut flowers arriving from a florist or home garden may also be a risk. See *Some toxic outdoor plants* (pp. 64–67) for common cutting flowers. Again, *this is a partial list.* Your local resources will provide more specific information for your region.

Symptoms of plant poisoning experienced by adults, children, or pets may range from a mild skin rash to burning and blistering of the skin; there may be pain and irritation of the mouth to swelling of the throat; an upset stomach, vomiting and diarrhea may be experienced; in severe cases, liver, kidney, or heart damage may occur. The extent of the poisoning may depend on the amount of plant ingested; in some cases, a small amount may cause no symptoms, while a larger amount will cause obvious distress. On the other hand, one or two seeds or leaves from a severely toxic plant may cause kidney failure and lead to death.

Every residential home should have an emergency plan for plant poisoning. The plant committee, neighborhood supervisor and neighborhood team members should discuss options, create a procedure document, and communicate its contents and location to all staff. Suggested steps to include in this plan include:

- If *any unusual symptoms* appear in residents, children or pets, determine if the affected individual had opportunity to ingest or come in contact with toxic plant material.

- Identify the suspect plant by *both* common and scientific name, if possible.

- If the situation appears life threatening, call 9-1-1 and then call the local poison control board for further information. If the symptoms are mild, follow instructions as indicated by the plant poisoning procedure you put in place.

Are the Plants and Tools Accessible to the Residents?

Residents need to be able to interact with the plants when the mood strikes. A resident's ability to independently inspect sprouting seeds, pick off dead leaves, or water a plant (whether it needs it or not) are actions staff cannot take for granted. Staff should be aware of hazards from cluttered floors, spills, and other obstacles between residents and the plants. Reaching plants is vital to encouraging resident spontaneity with indoor gardening activities.

Residents using walkers or wheelchairs need more room to maneuver. If chairs, tables, or other barriers are in the way, discouragement sets in quickly. Residents may perceive plant care as a task for staff only. Keeping pathways clear and plants accessible to residents will encourage them and their families to take part in plant care.

Plants must be positioned in a way that allows residents to work comfortably with them. Small to medium plants can be placed on shelving or window ledges, which will enable residents in wheelchairs, or those who need to be seated, to reach the greenery from the side. Better yet, additional shelves (with sturdy structural support) can be built beneath windows to allow residents in wheelchairs to roll under the shelves so they can face the plants.

It might also be possible to make certain tools available at all times. Small, lightweight watering cans kept half-filled for easy carrying; a trowel or small cultivating tool; a container of soil and some clean flowerpots arranged on the work table will encourage spontaneous involvement and may even entice a family member to help. Make tactful signs that ask gardeners to "please return tools when done" to help cut down on lost or mislaid items.

Tools for Resident Use

Meeting the residents' need involving various physical and medical challenges will encourage participation and reduce residents' feelings of helplessness. A resident planning session can be held to introduce tools and methods for easier indoor gardening. An occupational therapist or a representative of a tool company which specializes in adaptive tools can lead this session. Even local medical supply houses may have ideas for and/or catalogs showing ways to adapt tool handles.

If planter boxes or comfortable plant shelves are in place, the need for certain specialized tools will be reduced. If the residents will be tending to floor plants in large pots, tools with extension handles may be helpful to reach the soil.

All residents will benefit in some way from special tools and equipment such as:

- Small, easily held, well-balanced watering cans
- Padded, easily held, Velcro-strapped, and/or angled tool handles, and easily operated scissors or pruners
- Lightweight tools or, possibly, weighted tools
- Left-handed pruners and scissors
- Brightly painted and marked tool handles (e.g., yellow with black dots for visibility

while working or when left lying in a path or on a seat)

- Handles long enough to reach a floor plant from a wheelchair or while standing; or handles bent for comfort when reaching across a planter box
- Lightweight indoor watering wands
- Plant labels written in large, easy-to-read letters
- Lightweight flower pots
- Protective gardening gloves (for thorny or spiny plants, leather is best; to protect from blisters and dirt, cotton or vinyl gloves will do the job; to protect from moisture, plant secretions and residue, vinyl or latex gloves work best)
- Wheelchair friendly tool caddies: There are many versions of these, some of which resemble pockets and attach to the wheelchair's arms and hang either inside the seating area or outside vertical to the chair. Other versions are located beneath the seat as hanging bags or as shelves. The styles will depend on the resident's mobility and dexterity. Common caddies can be adapted for use while in a wheelchair (see pp. 75–76).

Animals, Birds, and Plants

As each Home plans and creates its interior gardens, the staff should consider the resident animals and birds (or potential of having them) of this growing environment. Houseplant poisoning of animals is usually not a major concern. However, indoor greenery must be chosen not only for the safety and benefit of the residents, but also for the safety of cats, dogs, birds, guinea pigs, rabbits, and other domesticated creatures which sooner or later may inhabit the Home.

It is easier to start the houseplant collection with nontoxic plants than it is to eliminate toxic plants that have been donated or purchased after the greening process has started. If some of the plants in the Home are considered toxic to animals or birds, the staff may choose to transfer those plants to areas not visited by the animals or to remove them entirely.

Choosing plants can be done enjoyably and correctly if the selection is shared with a knowledgeable staff member, volunteer, or a community expert, and routine factors are kept in mind. In addition to the basic needs of the plants, animals' roaming range and their sometimes uncanny abilities to reach plants known to be toxic must be considered. Do the animals have the run of the home, or can they be kept from areas where potentially harmful plants are located?

The degree of harmfulness of the plants is also an important point. In years past, poinsettias were thought to be highly toxic. It's now known that these popular Christmas plants are only mildly disturbing to the digestive system of animals that might nibble a few leaves or flowers. Poinsettia may cause rash, vomiting, or diarrhea in large quantities, but in small quantities may have no effect at all.

Some practical poisoning prevention for animals includes:

- Keep the animals occupied with their own toys or chewies. A bored pet will look for things to do; this boredom may include nibbling on houseplants.

- Try to keep an open space on each windowsill for access by the cats.

- Provide cats with their own pots of catnip or grass (i.e., rye, oat, wheat) to chew on. This is an easy crop for younger children to plant during intergenerational activities before the cats arrive.

- Using a hot pepper spray on leaves may discourage chewing of houseplants. Alternatively, if you have a seedling nibbler amongst the companion animals, plant some hot peppers. Hot pepper seedlings can be as hot as their future peppers. One nibble of these seedlings will usually break cats or other critters of grazing on houseplants.

- Use only nontoxic soap sprays on plants— both indoors and outdoors. If a professional landscape crew maintains a portion of either the indoor or outdoor plants, a discussion with these personnel about using soap spray to discourage insects may be helpful.

- Hang **toxic** plants out of reach whenever possible. If the plant committee decides to keep some plants considered **toxic** or **potentially toxic**, be certain the animals cannot reach them or that all staff is aware of the danger if animals or residents eat those plants. Try to choose plants that are nontoxic to animals as well.

- *Know emergency procedures in case an animal eats a toxic plant. Have your veterinarian's phone number handy at all times.*

Keep the greenery selection process as simple as possible. The list of plants found in *Table 2 Specific plants and their lighting needs* (pp. 36–37) contains greenery choices considered to be nontoxic to animals, birds, and humans, and are relatively easy to grow in a residential environment.

Regarding donated houseplants, it is very helpful if the scientific and the common names of the plants brought in by families or friends are known. Since there can be more than one common name for a houseplant, and different plants are sometimes known by the same name, the "Latin" botanical name is the only sure way to identify a plant. Find out that name. Ask a plant expert to correctly identify any unknown plant.

Local university agriculture departments and extension services usually maintain a list of plants specific to that region that are toxic to animals. A complete list of plants and herbs toxic to animals may be obtained for a fee from the ASPCA National Animal Poison Control Center (see p. 136).

Pepper Spray

to discourage insects and pets

4–5 cloves	garlic
1/4 cup	hot pepper sauce
2 drops	vegetable oil
3–5 drops	Ivory dish soap or Fels Naptha
1 cup	hot water

Mix ingredients in a blender. Pour into a covered container and let sit for a day. Strain solution through cheesecloth; add to a gallon of water. Apply to tops and bottoms of infested leaves (especially new growth tips) with a spray bottle.

An indoor pot of catnip or a few catnip plants growing in the outdoor garden can be dried for later use and may add more to the environment than just a cat snack. Most mature cats love to chew on and roll in this fragrant herb, and the cat's entertaining behavior will delight the residents. Encouraging cats to use the catnip as well as the pots of grass for their own purposes may distract them from the forbidden houseplants.

A note about animals and herbs: There are a growing number of veterinarians and herbalists who use natural, holistic, and homeopathic treatments for animals. Investigating these natural approaches might prove interesting to residents and staff. Check your local library for books and magazines that focus on this topic.

Intergenerational Activities

First impressions are very important. Children need to know who is in charge for what part of the activity. Teachers can explain this clearly to them. Residents will also need to understand what is expected of them when they interact with the children. After the plant activities person has discussed details with the teacher, he or she might want to have a brief orientation with the residents prior to the first interaction with the children.

The type of interaction between children, residents, and plants will depend largely on the age of the children. Activities can be an extension of the weekly indoor gardening process or a show-and-tell session based on a monthly theme. **Just remember to request and expect monthly planning time with the children's teacher** so that he or she can assist the Home's staff to present the activity appropriately. Depending on the situation, expenses and equipment may also be shared between the Home and the child day center or school.

Relationships between elders and children in a gardening setting were evaluated in a 1997 study conducted by Jack Kerrigan and Nancy Stevenson. This study focused on interactions between elders and youth in an intergenerational horticultural/gardening program. Among the conclusions drawn after twelve weeks of observation and documentation were the following: increased companionship

developed in most of the elder–child partnerships; careful planning and preparation of materials prior to the activity resulted in sustained child–elder interactions; an understanding of roles was gained by the elders and children as a result of their participating in the planning process and being informed about the program and its goals. Other observed behaviors between elders and children that increased over the time period were smiling, helping and speaking spontaneously and calmly, and the student expression of satisfaction, interest, and asking questions. It was also noted that (in this case) gardening activities with live material created more interest among the participants than did craft and dried plant activities. Rather than handing out materials to the elders and children prior to an activity, all items needed for the activity were placed in a box. This helped to maintain the flow of elder–child interactions.

In a similar manner, the developing relationships between the residents in a nursing home and the children who become part of the day-to-day gardening interactions will create positive reasons for all participants to attend the activities. Organization and consistency in the way staff conduct the sessions will build respect and confidence in the abilities of the Plant Care Team and Activities staff.

Suggested Approaches and Techniques

- Try to coordinate purchasing supplies between the Home and child daycare center or student classes.

- At the first meeting, use nametags for residents and children. Ask the teacher to explain to the children that (staff member's name) will be the teacher for the next activity and that they are to listen to him or her.

- Use the same basic order for each session; for instance: hang up coats, sit in circle, short exercise, project for the day, and snack.

- Vary routines with spontaneous interactions (e.g., picking bouquets of flowers and greenery, reading a story, birdwatching) with more detailed, planned activities (e.g., planting seeds, examining a shovel full of compost with a magnifying glass, making a scarecrow).

- Have materials ready to go before the children arrive.

- Keep the sessions short, depending on attention spans of both children and elders.

- The activity may be action-related (e.g., planting seeds, watering plants, arranging flowers, weeding) or object-related (e.g., leaf shapes, soil types, tools for the job).

- Form resident–children teams for activities and workstations, and maintain the same team members for each visit. This will encourage the development of relationships and familiarity between the residents and children.

- Work with groups of four to six; fewer, if possible. More than one workstation may be needed to avoid waiting, and to prevent children and residents from getting bored or restless. Consider whether a helper should be placed at each workstation.

- Plan with both children's and residents' abilities in mind.

- Consider child-sized tools (this can be a garden club or retail outlet donation).

- Research how-to books on children's gardening and intergenerational approaches.

- Use appropriate hand-washing techniques.

- Know safety and emergency procedures.

If the children are older (elementary-aged and above), they can help the residents and staff plan the topics for discussion or the gardening activity. This input will give the children a feeling of ownership and will motivate them to get their hands dirty. Teachers should be present for these planning sessions until the staff member conducting the activities is familiar with and comfortable directing the combined group. The **Gardening Calendar** (pp. 99–130) offers ideas for activities with children and residents. Suggested resources for planning intergenerational gardening activities appear in the references (p. 133).

What Do the Residents Want?

Staff will discover that residents join in the greenery activities in their own way and in their own time. Participation will depend on the resident's background, physical and mental abilities, general attitudes, and very importantly, the enthusiasm of the Plant Care Team and others who coordinate the greenery interactions.

Encouraging and Empowering Residents and Families

Encouraging the residents to take ownership of personal plants in their own rooms or to become involved in plant care in the common living areas can be a challenge. At first there will be only a handful of residents who are actually willing to get dirt under their fingernails or who want to water the plants. This is a normal reaction. After all, they've worked all their lives, are now retired, and are paying for their daily care.

Staff might get the ball rolling by describing to the residents what Eden Alternative Homes are doing with indoor plants. The Eden Alternative web site lists nursing homes and assisted living homes that are certified as Eden Alternative sites along with the Homes' progress stories. Consider reading a few of these stories at resident meetings.

A topic for a resident meeting entitled *How the indoor plants take care of people* might be of interest to the more skeptical residents and staff. Not every person living or working in the Home is going to get excited about growing night blooming cereus or watching a sensitive plant collapse when touched. For those residents who respond with the attitude "Who wants a jungle in here, anyway?" presenting the practical benefits of having plants might carry some weight.

Empower the residents by making them feel that their input is important to the creation of their indoor gardening environment. It will go a long way in motivating them to take part in the care of the greenery. Some suggestions to help the residents feel their input is valued include:

- Have a notebook handy and write down resident suggestions; let the residents see you taking notes.

- Ask residents to name or describe indoor plants from their childhood.

- Show residents pictures of nontoxic plants that are ideal for their surroundings; ask them which kind they would prefer.

- Make herb bread with a breadmaker. Use fresh herbs from the supermarket, the garden, or indoor pots to show residents examples of plants that can be grown inside for culinary uses.

- Ask residents for ideas about how to use plants in other ways (e.g., gifts to welcome new residents, as conversation pieces for visiting family, friends and grandchildren, as gifts to give to family, food for indoor pets).

- Discuss where the residents want to locate the plants. Include in this discussion the importance of ideal locations for each plant.

- Invite family members to these discussion meetings; serve herb bread.

- Promote a Resident Plant Care Volunteer program. Hold mini training sessions and explain tasks such as removing dead leaves, cleaning plant leaves, cultivating soil, watering plants, and cleaning trash out of plant pots. Assign plants to each resident. Attendees may receive a "Plant Care Team Volunteer" button or nametag.

Planning Resident Garden Appreciation Groups (Garden Clubs)

Residents and staff need a scheduled time to come together as a gardening group. Even though plants are a part of the Home's environment and are accessible at any time, the residents and Plant Care Team need time to interact and plan in a more organized fashion. This meeting gives each participant a voice in the planning, and a variety of ideas and approaches can be presented.

The participants can decide on their leadership. It might be a resident, a member of the Plant Team, or a cochair arrangement with the staff member doing the bulk of the physical preparations. Residents may also decide to leave all of the responsibility with the staff members.

Suggested discussion topics:

- How often to meet, where, and for how long

- What is the purpose of the group? (e.g., educational, opportunity to work with plants, hear outside speakers, express opinions about the indoor greenery, suggest new varieties of plants)

- Who prepares the agenda?

- Who arranges materials, furniture, and other supplies or equipment for the meeting?

- Who cleans up afterward?

- Will refreshments be served?

Workspace for Residents, Staff and Plants

Finding a corner where transplanting and other comfortable plant puttering can be done may require some creative rearranging or designing. Having a designated space for staff and residents to work at their leisure with nearby shelf space for a few tools and pots will encourage spontaneous participation, and eliminate the need to prepare and/or clean up a dining room table. In this situation, garden and civic club connections and resulting donations can be very helpful for funding materials. The creative talents of the Plant Committee members can also be invaluable at this time.

A six-foot cafeteria-style table is probably adequate, but a custom-designed potting table can be built at little cost. Ask your maintenance department committee member to look around in the garage and storage areas for materials suitable for recycling. Be sure the table can accommodate wheelchairs at a comfortable height, has no sharp edges, and has a nonporous surface. On either the cafeteria table or the homemade table, a three-sided box with two sloping sides can be installed at one end for holding soil mix and for easy cleanup with a whisk broom. A hinged lid on the box will prevent the soil from drifting onto the table.

Selecting New Plants for Indoor Use

Once the plants already living at the residence are spruced up and rearranged, the fun of selecting, soliciting, and seeking new and interesting houseplants can begin. Remember that a feeling of ownership of the indoor environment among the residents, their families, and the staff contributes greatly to the desire to care for the plants. Be sure to involve these people in the planning and donating aspects of the indoor greenery.

Before announcing the need for plants, have the following information available:

- Decide where more plants are needed/wanted in each neighborhood and in the public areas.

- Refer to *Table 2 Light needs of common houseplants* (pp. 36–37). All of the plants in this table are selected from the **nontoxic** and **potentially toxic** list. Match the plants to their ideal location (light exposure).

- Determine what kinds of containers new plants need (e.g., pot and saucer, hanging basket, wall bracket, large floor pot, planter box). The purchase of the final containers can be done later.

- Remember that several smaller plants with similar lighting and watering needs can be combined in one pot.

- Determine if drip saucers are available or needed. Will these be included in the donations, or will a staff member be purchasing coordinated pots for the new plants?

Create an **Indoor Plant Donation Request** form specific to each resident floor, neighborhood, and public area and post it for donors and staff. Have **Donor Forms** available for family, friends and visitors to take with them. To prevent duplication of plant donations, ask the donor to indicate which plant(s) he or she intends to donate. These plant names can then be removed temporarily from the master guide until the plants are brought to the Home by the donor. The donor forms should be returned with the donated plants, placed in a plastic resealable bag, and fastened with a rubber band to the plant label stuck in the soil. These forms can be referred to when placing plants in the correct location. These forms might also be kept as references for sending thank-you notes. See Figures 2 and 3 (pp. 30, 31). There are also fill-in-the-blank versions in the appendix (pp. 138, 139).

The source of the indoor plants might be a family member's houseplant collection, a local florist, a greenhouse, or a mail-order supply company. The plant committee might want to discuss adding names and addresses of recommended local retail florists and greenhouses who practice organic methods to the donation forms. The donation guides and forms will keep the donors on track while selecting safe and appropriate plants.

There are additional ways to acquire new indoor plants. If the Home's budget allows, the plant committee can decide which types of plants they want and locations, and the greenery can then be purchased with the help of the houseplant mentor. The community-at-large can become involved through presentations to garden clubs and civic groups by developing a similar Indoor Plant Donation Request and Donor Form to organize donations from these sources.

Receiving Donated Plants; Holding a "Plant Donation Day"

As families, friends, and community organizations become familiar with your gardening plans, they will want to know how they can help. One vital way is by contributing houseplants, either from healthy home stock, or by direct purchase from a reputable grower or distributor. Another way to help is through monetary contribution to purchase plants from catalogs, and to buy plant containers, hardware to hang plants, or plant stands. The plant committee will need to coordinate container and hardware purchases for color and style. See *Selecting pots and containers* (p. 32).

When the plant committee and Plant Care Teams have decided what plants they need and where to place them, they can post their Indoor Plant Donations Request and accept plants for a set period of time, or hold a Plant Donation Day. Prior to this day, a similar guide can be posted; add the time, date, and location for dropping off plants.

Plan the Donation Day during warmer weather to avoid damage to the plants being transported to the Home. Arrange the day with the houseplant mentor and have volunteers on hand to transplant the donations into their new containers

Indoor Plant Donation Request

The residents of Shady Grove are very happy to accept your gifts of live plants and blooming flowers to enhance our resident areas. Please make your selection(s) from the list below and obtain a **donor form**. To prevent duplications, please notify a staff member of your choices prior to purchase. We have the following requests for this living area:

Unit Name: FRIENDLY ACRE

Location for Plants: Hall window next to room #1228

Exposure: East, natural light

Our Plant Choices

TYPE OF PLANT	POT SIZE	NUMBER WANTED
African Violet (*Saintpaulia*) **or** Angel Wing Begonia (any variety or color)	4–6 inch pot with saucer	(1)
Swedish Ivy (*Plectranthus australis*), Prayer Plant (*Maranta leuconeura*) **or** *Peperomia* (any variety or color)	6 inch hanging pot with attached drip saucer	(1)
Lady Palm (*Rhapis excelsa*) **or** Bamboo Palm (*Chamaedorea seifrizii*)	8–10 inch with saucer	(1)

Additional Needs: Monetary donations for hanging plant hardware, pots, and plant stands.

NOTE TO DONORS:

Please include a label for each plant with its common and botanical name if possible. The plants should be kept in the pots in which they were purchased. If saucers are not attached, please include a clear plastic saucer one size larger than the pot. Thank you.

If you have any questions, please call: Sandy Garner 555–2163

Figure 2   **Sample Indoor Plant Donation Request Flyer**

Indoor Plant Donor Form

The residents of Shady Grove are very happy to accept your gifts of live plants and flowers to enhance our resident areas. **Please CIRCLE your selection(s) from the list below. To prevent duplications, please notify a staff member of your choices prior to purchase. We have the following requests for this living area:**

Unit Name: FRIENDLY ACRE

Location for Plants: Hall window next to room #1228

Exposure: East, natural light

PLANT CHOICES

TYPE OF PLANT	POT SIZE	NUMBER WANTED
African Violet (Saintpaulia) **or** Angel Wing Begonia (any variety or color)	4–6 inch pot with saucer	(1)
Swedish Ivy (Plectranthus australis), Prayer Plant (Maranta leuconeura) **or** Peperomia (any variety or color)	6 inch hanging pot with attached drip saucer	(1)
Lady Palm (Rhapis excelsa) **or** Bamboo Palm (Chamaedorea seifrizii)	8–10 inch with saucer	(1)

Additional Needs: Monetary donations for hanging plant hardware, pots, and plant stands.

NOTE TO DONORS:

Please include a **label with the common and botanical name for each plant** if possible. The plants should be kept in the pots in which they were purchased. If saucers are not attached, please include a clear plastic saucer one size larger than the pot. Thank you.

Please return this form with the plant(s) or monetary donation.

NAME OF DONOR: _____

ADDRESS: _____

_____

If you have any questions, please call: *Sandy Garner 555-2163*

Figure 3   Sample Donor Form

and deliver plants to the resident, floor, or public area. Ask volunteers to arrive a half-hour early for transplanting instructions. These volunteers may be residents, so have a worktable and chairs set up for anyone who needs to sit comfortably or who uses a wheelchair.

Consider sending a **news release** to the local newspaper, radio, and/or television stations. Include all pertinent info a couple of weeks before the event. A week or so before Plant Donation Day, volunteers and any other individuals or groups can be asked to donate, loan, or bring along as many of the following supplies as possible. Have these ready in the plant donation workroom:

❑ At least two cafeteria-style tables, covered with a plastic tarp for easy clean up, one for setting donated plants on, and the other for workspace.

❑ Sterile potting soil mix (a commercial mixture specifically for indoor plants; often called a "soilless mix" since it contains a variety of ingredients but no soil)

❑ Extra containers and pots of varying sizes, either new, color-coordinated pots, or utility pots and saucers. Used pots are fine as long as they've been washed in a bleach solution (see p. 45).

❑ Plant labels, wax pencils, indelible markers and clear nail polish, or a label maker

❑ Trowels, gloves (latex, cotton, and vinyl), rags

❑ Watering cans

❑ Plant cart with supplies

❑ Houseplant reference books

❑ Dust brush and pan, vacuum cleaner

❑ Toxic plant lists; include photos if plant expert not available

❑ Refreshments

Using the Indoor Plants Donor Form accompanying the donated plants, place the plants in groups according to the selected locations indicated on the forms. Then evaluate the plants for the presence of disease and insects, identify them as nontoxic or potentially toxic, and label each plant with common and botanical names. Plants can be transplanted as needed, then taken to the prechosen area, and watered there. If disease or insects are suspected, or the plant cannot be identified, isolate these plants for treatment and/or further research.

The plant committee may want to hold a **fundraising event** to raise money for additional plants or containers. After the Plant Donation Day is over, the committee may wish to announce a "money only" donation request for purchasing specific plants. Mention their cost, and where they will be located within the nursing home.

Other options include contacting local nurseries and specialty plant societies. **Local nurseries** or greenhouses may be willing to purchase plants for the Home from a supplier of unusual or exotic plants and sell them at a **discounted rate**. The Home might have to agree to buy a certain number of plants to get a discount.

Specialty plant societies may offer deals on unusual plants. Ask your local **botanical garden** for names and numbers of people to contact. Find the book, *Gardening by Mail* (Barton, 1997) for a list of sources for many plants, seed companies, associations, garden supplies, and much more.

Regardless of the way in which the plants are obtained, the process is an ongoing and enjoyable one. As new plants grow, cuttings or divisions can be taken, and the starter plants added to the Home's environment, offered to a donor as a thank-you, or traded with a hobby grower for a new variety.

Selecting Pots and Containers

It goes without saying that time, effort, and finances are being invested in the building of the indoor gardening environment. Along with the consideration of the tremendous overall benefits that indoor greenery will bring to residents, don't forget visual impressions. The general appearance of the plants and their containers do make a difference. The plant committee will want to provide guidance for a well-coordinated, easily maintained, and attractive plant display. The Plant Care Team will be rewarded with sturdy and visually pleasing pots. The residents and families will be uplifted by inviting surroundings.

As with all of the planning phases for the indoor gardening environment, include the residents in the discussion about selecting new plant containers. Each resident neighborhood may want a different color for its own indoor garden areas. The Plant Committee can narrow down the container style choices to simplify the process. Remember that quantity purchasing of pots may lower the individual price.

If a Home has the luxury of a contracted interior decorator or interior plant maintenance company and the budget to purchase coordinating plant containers, the plant committee and team(s) will have a pleasant time introducing the decorator to their indoor greenery. On the other hand, if this is a do-it-yourself operation, the following suggestions may be helpful.

- Buy pots locally, a few at a time, from garden and home supply stores.

- Check additional choices in garden center catalogs.

- Try buy-out stores for real bargains.

- Inquire about discounts if larger quantities are ordered.

- Create a nostalgic containers and plants display by using unusual or old-time pots and containers which can be donated by families and friends.

- Ask for volunteer advice from a reputable local interior designer or interior landscaping company.

Containers come in many styles, colors, and materials. Here are some pointers:

- **Clay pots:** Advantages include a natural appearance and a porous composition that allows water to evaporate through the pot for cacti and other plants needing drier soil. Disadvantages are weight, fragility, they stain easily, and it's difficult to keep soil evenly moist.

- **Glazed ceramic containers** are colorful and clean easily. Disadvantages are that they are heavy and breakable.

- **Plastic pots** are durable, lightweight, and easily washed, but can sometimes crack.

Pots can also come equipped with a variety of **saucers**. Some examples are:

- Attached saucer fits flush with base of pot; however, it may be difficult to see standing water or to remove water.

- Saucer which stands away from base of pot; standing water can be seen.

- No saucer, self-watering style: holds supply of water which is used by the plant as needed; reduces the frequency of watering.

The pot into which a plant is directly placed *must* have drainage holes to prevent water from accumulating around the roots and causing root rot. The plant can be placed directly into the decorative pot, and set on a saucer, or planted in a black plastic utility pot that is then set down into a decorative pot. In order to promote good drainage with black utility pots, bricks, pebbles, or sturdy pieces of styrofoam may be placed in the bottom of the decorative pot to elevate the black pot above any standing water.

Anything watertight may be used as a decorative container as long as the potted plant is in a pot with drainage holes. Residents may have favorite pots they want to use for their personal plants (e.g., china chamber pots, brass spittoons, kitchen bowls). The Plant Team may have to hunt for the best utility pot to fit such unusual containers. One-of-a-kind containers are great, and may help motivate residents to participate.

If a planter box is in place or is to be built, be sure it receives sufficient light from overhead fluorescent lights or a window within three feet of the box. Decide what height the plants will be and consider the size of the pots. The box can be fitted with a galvanized or aluminum tray deep enough to hold various sized pots. To keep the plants out of standing water, Rodale's *Encyclopedia of Indoor Gardening* suggests using a cut-to-size, egg crate diffuser grid as found in ceiling lights. The maintenance department will know how to fit this.

Soil for Indoor Plants

There are many brands of indoor potting soil on the market, but not every type of potting soil is appropriate for all plants. A soil that is lightweight, sterile, and composed of a mixture of organic materials is preferred. Consider these options:

- Soil mixed for foliage plants may be composed of perlite, vermiculite, ground bark, peat moss, and possibly sand. **Peat is not potting soil.**

- Read the label and note the plants that are recommended for that soil.

- Many commercial soils contain fertilizer. This is convenient; just remember not to use additional fertilizer for the recommended period of time.

- Cheap soil is usually not high quality.

- Soils for cacti and succulents are a separate mix, as are growing mediums for orchids and African violets.

- If in doubt, call a Master Gardener or ask a greenhouse grower.

- Soil from an outside garden is *never* acceptable for indoor plants—it's heavy, does not drain well, and contains insects and their eggs.

Indoor Plants and Lighting

Long-term care homes often lack the perfect window light for growing plants. When rearranging existing plants and choosing new ones, the various light exposures (compass points of north, south, east, and west) as well as artificial lighting must be considered.

A complete, indoor houseplant book will provide the staff with most of the lighting requirement information for properly locating each plant. If a particular plant's name is not listed or the plant mentor is not able to identify the plant, it can be placed in an eastern window and observed for growth response.

Affects of Low Light and Too Much Light

If the **light is too low** for a plant, the following distress signs may be seen:

- Spindly new leaf growth
- New leaves pale; older leaves yellowing
- Blackening of leaf tips
- Soil not drying out between watering
- Drooping or dropping leaves
- Overall growth slow or no growth at all
- Other plants in the immediate area doing well

On the other hand, **too much light** may result in the following distress signals:

- "Sunburned" leaves (light brown streaks or patches)
- Dried, brown leaf edges
- Bleaching out of natural color
- Wilting (even when soil is moist)

Time and experience are good teachers of the effects of too little or too much light. Be certain the problem is not insect or disease damage, then move the distressed plant to a different light exposure or increase the amount of artificial light. Gradually increase or decrease the plant's proximity to the light source. Sometimes the shade of another light-loving plant will protect one that doesn't like direct sun. For plants that need brighter light, a few inches closer to the window can mean the difference between richly colored flowers and boring, green foliage.

Coverings at windows, even a sheer curtain, will reduce the amount of light considerably. This might be good for a low-light plant but not healthy for one which needs higher light levels.

Look for roof overhangs, decorative trim, large trees or canopies that shade windows. These can reduce the light needed to keep begonias and jasmine blooming or herbs sturdy and strong. Be aware of the difference between a tree in winter without leaves and that same tree in the midsummer.

If a Home is fortunate enough to have a large, southern exposure window, with no light-reducing outside obstacles, and space to display or grow plants, much can be done with that setting. Flowers will bloom, several varieties of herbs can be grown, and even seedlings will do well.

Many enjoyable plants will thrive in eastern, western, and northern windows, especially with a little additional encouragement. Inexpensive mirrors placed to catch the light and reflect it back on the plants will increase the ability for plants to grow. White or pastel wall colors help reflect light. A fluorescent light fixture located in the ceiling directly above the plants will maintain certain foliage plants in a low-light window. When a fluorescent light fixture is hung approximately 6–12 inches above plants (as on a shelf or special plant box unit) flowering plants (e.g., orchids, begonias, African violets) and easy-care, colorful foliage plants (e.g., prayer plants, beefsteak plants, coleus) can be grown successfully.

Newly sprouted seedlings require bright southern light, but will do best under an artificial light left on 12–14 hours a day. See *Starting seeds indoors*, p. 72.

Specific Plants and Their Lighting Needs

It is likely that Homes will have a number of plants that are **potentially toxic** to animals, and possibly to people. The more common **potentially toxic** plant varieties have been included in Table 2 (pp. 36–37) to give the plant committee a frame of reference for taking appropriate action. Give serious consideration before rearranging or bringing in these varieties of plants. A more complete list of plants potentially toxic to animals is found in the ASPCA's *Household Plant Reference*.

Retiring Silk and Plastic Plants

Many nursing homes and similar residential facilities have been attractively decorated with silk plants and trees at a considerable cost to the owners. What can be done with these lovely but nonliving items when the live greenery of the indoor garden habitat begins to arrive?

The kindest position to take would be one of relocation. There are always dark halls and corners where living plants cannot survive, or where a touch of color would be welcome. The presence of **plastic** plants, however, cannot be tolerated. By gradually removing all silk plants from prominent entryways and resident areas, and by replacing them with appropriate live greenery, the vibrant and growing environment will be represented accurately.

If there are too many silk plants to relocate within the Home, the Home might consider having a quiet, in-house sale for employees and families, or donating the plants to a nonresidential agency.

Table 2   Light Needs of Common Houseplants

NORTH or LOW LIGHT or NO WINDOW LOCATIONS: Ceiling fluorescent light is necessary if the window has any outside obstructions. If there is only a ceiling light unit, it must be left on at least 12 hours each day with the plant placed directly beneath it on the floor or a table.

COMMON NAME	SCIENTIFIC NAME	TOXICITY
Cast iron plant	Aspidistra	Nontoxic
Holly fern	Cyrtonmium falcatum	Non
Kentia palm	Howea	Non
Mother-in-law's tongue, Snake plant	Sansevieria, any type	Potentially
Nerve plant	Fittonia verschaffeltii	Non
Norfolk Island pine	Araucaria heterophylla	Potentially
Parlor palm	Chamaedorea elegans	Non
Peperomia (Watermelon, plain green, varigated)	Peperomia argyreia, P. obtusifolia	Non
Prayer plant	Maranta leuconeura	Non
Rabbit's foot fern	Davallia	Non
Spider plant	Chlorophytum comosum	Non
Strawberry begonia	Saxifraga stolonifera	Non
Wandering Jew, varigated	Tradescantia fluminensis	Potentially
Wandering Jew, purple	T. Zebrina pendula	Potentially
*Weeping fig,	Ficus benjamina,	Potentially
*Indian laurel	F. retusa nitida	Potentially

* Caution advised with any variety due to potential toxicity.

EASTERN or WESTERN WINDOW LOCATIONS: This may be direct sunshine for two or more hours, or bright indirect light. Some plants may be sensitive to direct afternoon sun.

COMMON NAME	SCIENTIFIC NAME	TOXICITY
Areca palm	Chrysalidocarpus lutescens	Potentially
Bamboo palm	Chamaedorea seifrizii	Non
Basil	Several varieties	Non
Bay	Laurus Nobilis	Non
Beefsteak plant, Blood leaf	Iresine herbstii	Non
Begonia (Angel wing, Tuberous, Rex, Wax)	According to variety	Non
Burnet	Poterium sanguisorba	Non
Chervil	Anthriscis cerefolium	Non
Chocolate soldier plant	Episcia dianthiflora	Non
Christmas cactus (several types)	Schlumbergera russeliana, Zygocactus truncatus	Potentially
Flowering Maple	Abutilon	Non
(Summer exposure: at least 4 hours of direct morning sun; Winter: move to southern window)		
Geranium (flowering and scented)	According to variety	Potentially
Grape ivy, Oak leaf ivy	Cissus rhombifolia	Non
Hoya, Wax plant, Porcelain flower	Hoya carnosa	Non
Kentia palm (no direct sun)	Howea	Non
Lady's ear drops	Fushcia	Non
Lady palm	Rhapis excelsa	Non
Lemon verbena	Aloysia triphylla	Non
Lipstick plant	Aeschynanthus pulcher	Non
Mints (several varieties)	Mentha	Non
Mosaic vase	Gusmania lingulata	Non
Night blooming cereus	Hylocereus undatus	Non

Table 2	Light Needs of Common Houseplants (continued)

EASTERN or WESTERN WINDOW LOCATIONS (continued)

COMMON NAME	SCIENTIFIC NAME	TOXICITY
Norfolk Island pine	Auraucaria	Potentially
Parlor palm	Chamaedorea elegans	Non
Pearl plant	Haworthia subfaciata	Non
Peperomia (several varieties)	According to variety	Non
Piggy-back plant	Tolmiea menziesii	Non
Polka dot plant	Hypoestes sanguinolenta	Non
Pony tail palm	Beucarnea recurvata	Non
Prayer plant	Maranta leuconeura	Non
Purple passion plant	Gynura aurantiaca	Non
Rabbit's foot fern (east)	Davilla	Non
Rosemary	Rosmarius officinalis	Non
Schefflera, Umbrella tree	Brassaia actinophylla	Potentially
Sensitive plant (prefers 4 hours of full sun)	Mimosa pudica	Non
Spider plant	Chlorophytum comosum	Non
Star jasmine (west)	Trachelospermum jasminoides	Non
Strawberry begonia (east)	Saxifraga stolonifera	Non
Swedish ivy	Plectranthus australis	Non
Wandering Jew (purple and varigated; may be sensitive to full sun)	Tradescantia fluminensis, Zebrina pendula	Potentially Potentially
Weeping fig (all varieties)	According to variety	Potentially
Yucca, Palm lily (prefers 3 hours of direct sun)	Yucca elephantipes	Non

SOUTHERN WINDOW LOCATION: These are often blooming plants, herbs, desert plants, and seedlings.

COMMON NAME	SCIENTIFIC NAME	TOXICITY
Basil	Ocimum, many varieties	Non
Begonia (Angel wing, fibrous, rex, wax)	According to variety	Non
Beefsteak plant	Iresine herbstii	Non
Coriander	Coriandrum sativum	Non
Dill	Anethum graveolens	Non
Flowering maple (winter exposure)	Abutilon	Non
Geranium (flowering and scented varieties)	Pelargonium	Potentially
Glory bower	Clerodendrum Thomsoniae	Non
Marjoram	Origanum majorana	Non
Mints (several varieties)	Mentha	Non
Nasturtium	Tropaeolum minus	Non
Night blooming cereus	Hylocereus undatus	Non
Oregano	Origanum	Non
Paper plant (thorns)	Bougainvillea	Potentially
Parsley	Petroselinum crispum	Non
Polka dot plant	Hypoestes	Non
Pony tail palm	Beucarnea recurvata	Non
Pot marigold	Calendula officinalis	Non
Rosemary	Rosmarius	Non
Sage	Salvia officinalis	Non
Star jasmine	Trachelospermum jasminoides	Non
Summer savory	Satureja hortensis	Non
Turf lily	Liriope muscari	Non
Winter savory	Satureja montana	Non
Yucca, Palm lily	Yucca elephatipes	Non

Part 2: Digging In

Caring for Indoor Plants

Enjoyable plant care happens when the Plant Care Team has a base for operations. That base can be a closet, a shelf, or the plant cart. Adequate and *secure* space to store tools and equipment used for weekly plant maintenance is essential. Be sure that supervisors and staff are aware of and in agreement with the Plant Care Team using that space, and that all items are clearly labeled.

Every Plant Care Person will develop his or her own methods as the plants and their individual needs become familiar. The following **plant care guidelines** will help new team members get into a routine, and will provide seasoned members with some new approaches.

Putting It All Together

A checklist of plant care will help the Team enjoy what they're doing and do it faster. Try the following before starting plant care:

- ❏ Have the plant cart stocked and ready to go each week.
- ❏ Ask for volunteer resident helpers, schedule them in advance, give them a copy of the schedule, and the plant care checklist.
- ❏ Invite a more confused resident, just before starting plant care, to join the Plant Care Person.
- ❏ Review with resident (prior to plant care day) what he or she will be doing in plant care such as watering, grooming, and inspecting, or ask the resident to discuss what portion of care he or she wants to do.

Then try using these **steps for weekly plant maintenance:**

- ❏ While using the plant cart, place it out of the resident and staff traffic pattern.
- ❏ Rotate the plant pot approximately ¼ turn to the right (clockwise).
- ❏ Cultivate the soil. The plant label in small pots may be used as a digger.

- ❏ Check soil for moisture using your finger first for pots of 6-inch diameter or smaller, and a water meter for larger pots.
- ❏ Water (if needed).
- ❏ Groom, clean, and inspect plant.
- ❏ Clean pot or container side that is most visible.
- ❏ Check pot saucer or bottom of decorative container for standing water.
- ❏ Pour out or syringe excess water into an empty bucket. Don't reuse water with other plants. Reusing water encourages disease and insects.
- ❏ Clean the floor around the plant.
- ❏ Make a notation on the plant care sheet for each plant or area.

Watering Plants

When to Water

Check each plant weekly or more frequently if the leaves begin to wilt before the week is over. Check the soil in small pots with your index finger. Sink your finger into soil as far as possible. If soil is dry as far down as the finger can detect, water **is** needed with the exception of cacti which may not need water until a slight shriveling of the leaves is noticed. A water meter for checking larger pots will be helpful since moisture is present below the finger tip depth.

Other signs or conditions that indicate a need for water include:

- Leaves are limp, stems bent; soil has shrunken away from sides of pot; soil is cracked.
- Days are getting longer; days have been bright and sunny; additional fans are operating or windows are open; the routine watering day was missed due to illness or short staffing.

When NOT to Water

- If the soil is cool and damp on and below the surface, *no* water is needed.
- If soil is dry on the surface, and damp below the surface, *no* water needed.

Other situations where watering might ***not*** be needed at the scheduled time:

- Days are short and cloudy (e.g., during winter).
- Temperature in the Home has been cooler (especially where air conditioning hits plants).
- Leaves have filled out on the trees outside and have reduced light in the windows where plants are located (e.g., spring and summer).
- A new awning or construction-in-progress has shaded a formerly sunny window.
- Helpful residents have watered before the plant care person got there.

How Much Water?

Before watering, stir (cultivate) soil surface slightly, especially if no mulch is being used, if the soil is hard and dry, if the soil has pulled away from sides of pot, or if mold is present on soil surface. Use a small digging tool; wipe off tools with rubbing alcohol before using it with another plant. If the soil is soft, the plant label can be used to cultivate.

- Fill pot to brim with water, let it soak in. Do this up to two times, covering the entire surface of the soil with water. Observe for water draining into saucer. If no drainage appears, water again.
- If in doubt about a plant's need for water, wait a day then check the plant again.
- It's always *better* to **underwater** than it is to overwater.
- Remove any standing water in saucers if not absorbed by the next day.

Cleaning (Grooming) Plants

- ❏ Clean portion of plant facing out (area most visible).
- ❏ Snip off any yellowing or dead leaves, and plant parts.
- ❏ Clip dead twigs and branches.
- ❏ Remove old blossoms.
- ❏ Spray a feather duster with soap spray from the spray bottle. Brush backs and tops of leaves and stems starting with the upper branches and working down toward bottom of the plant.

Inspecting Plants

As the plants are being groomed, give each one a good visual inspection. Look for the following signs of trouble and these possible causes:

- **Yellowing leaves at the base of the plant** may be caused by overwatering, low light, or poor air circulation.

Soap Spray

to discourage insects

| 1–2 tablespoons | Ivory dish soap or Fels Naptha |
| 1 gallon | warm water |

Dissolve soap in warm water; allow to cool. Fill spray bottle. Spray a feather duster with the solution and brush the tops and bottoms of the leaves starting with the upper branches and working down toward the bottom of the plant.

- **Droopy, limp leaves, even after watering** may be caused by overwatering (root and stem rotting).

- **Leaves full on one side, skimpy on the other** may be caused by uneven light (plant not being turned).

- **Brown, crispy leaf tips or black soft tips** may be stress from too little or too much water, or too much fertilizer.

- **Brown or pale circular spots** forming on leaves may be caused by overwatering, or indicate spread of disease.

- **White fuzzy covering or brown mushy spots** on leaves or stems may be caused by the use of nonsterile soil, poor air circulation, or indicate spread of disease.

- **Regular dust buildup** on leaves. Guess what? This is *normal.*

- **Soggy soil before watering** may be caused by low light or temperature, root rot, a helpful resident, or the bottom of pot left sitting in water.

- **Accumulations of orange-brown, grayish white coating** on surface of soil may be caused by overwatering, poor air circulation, or use of nonsterile soil.

- **Tiny moving specks** on under side of leaves indicates spider mites usually from dry air.

- **Sticky spots and/or webbing** under and on top of leaves may indicate spider mites or aphids from dry air or nearby plants.

- **Small, brown scalelike growths** on stems or leaves; indicates scale insects.

- **Small, slow moving insects** on new growth tips of plant indicates aphids.

- **White, cottony, sticky masses** indicates mealy bugs.

- Clouds of **white flying insects**; white flies.

- **Dark-colored flying insects:** Most likely fungus gnats. These are usually found when the soil isn't sterile, when outdoor soil is introduced into pots, or when a plant is donated from a home environment. These insects are annoying, but not especially damaging.

The majority of these problems can be prevented or controlled by good care practices and careful inspection of new plants arriving at the Home. Early detection and treatment of insects and disease usually keeps any problem from getting out of hand.

Controlling Creepy Crawlies and Plant Diseases

The Plant Committee will need to discuss the use of natural and/or chemical treatment of insects and diseases. In any residential setting, **only** *the use of natural treatment for indoor and outdoor plants is encouraged.* The presence of many people and animals in close contact with these plants is reason enough to use methods that would reduce or eliminate the possibility of harmful reactions to liquids or other substances used to treat the greenery.

In the previous section *Inspecting the plants,* a variety of insect and disease indicators was reviewed. A number of preventative steps can be taken to reduce or eliminate the possibility of these pests. The first line of defense is **good plant care practices**. Here are some suggestions:

❏ *Universal precautions* apply to plants too! Wash tools and hands with soap and water before and after each plant care session. Wipe off tools used before going to another plant. Clean tools and hands with alcohol if contagious plant disease or insect infestation is suspected. Bag up severely infected plants immediately and discard in dumpster unless the plant has a personal value to a resident. Isolate plants which have a mild case of disease or insects.

❏ Use sterilized soil only.

❏ Discuss concerns and show examples of problem plants to the residents.

❏ Ask for their advice and observation.

❏ Communicate plant care concerns to other Neighborhood Team members and to the houseplant mentor.

❏ Water soil only—not leaves.

❏ **Don't overwater.**

❏ Provide good air circulation. Use a small fan if necessary.

❏ Provide good soil drainage with bricks, styrofoam pieces, or pebbles in bottom of decorative pots to raise the bottom of inner pots above the water level, and by timely removal of standing water.

❏ Place plants in appropriate lighting and temperature conditions.

❏ Be aware of temperature changes. Hot, dry conditions can promote pests. Cold soil encourages mold and root rot.

❏ Keep soil absorbent by mulching or cultivating as needed.

❏ To prevent resident cats from using the soil, spread mulch on the soil surface or hang the plants out of feline reach.

❏ Provide additional humidity by grouping plants or encourage it through water evaporation from a pebble base.

❏ Feed foliage plants on a regular schedule. Use half as much of the recommended amount of fertilizer half as often. Fertilize only during the growing season (early spring through fall) unless you are using a time-release fertilizing soil or pellets. For some flowering plants, such as African violets and orchids, specific fertilizers are available and the fertilizing schedule may vary.

❏ Buy plants known to be resistant to insects and diseases.

Natural Treatment for Insects

A number of interesting concoctions for discouraging insect pests exist. The most easily prepared is a soap spray. However, even mild sprays can have damaging effects on certain types of houseplants. Do not use household soap sprays on euphorbias (e.g., croton, crown of thorns, poinsettia), ferns, or any fuzzy-leafed plant. Be sure to treat plants in a shaded area since soap sprays may cause sunburn damage. Read the labels for precautions involving specific types of plants.

Mix 1–2 tablespoons of Ivory dish soap or Fels Naptha in a gallon of warm water. When insects are seen and identified, spray the plant thoroughly, especially at the leaf tips, underneath the leaves, and in stem and branch notches. Use a feather duster sprayed with the soap solution to brush off these areas and dislodge insects. Treatment may need to be repeated once a day for 2–3 days until no insect movement is detected.

Commercially sold insecticidal soap sprays (e.g., Safer's) are made from fatty acids and are generally less harmful to plants than household soaps. They do not harm beneficial insects, and are effective at controlling the majority of common houseplant pests. Look for this type of spray in catalogs and at garden centers.

Another effective approach is to use a dormant oil spray (also known as lightweight summer oil). This is safe to use around humans, but might be messy. As with the soap sprays, take care not to use on orchids or other epiphytic plants (e.g., air ferns), ferns, and fuzzy-leafed plants. Check with greenhouses or greenhouse supply stores.

When using any type of spray, other than plain water, be certain residents, children, animals, and other staff are not in the line of fire. **Spraying should be done by the Plant Care Team only and the solution locked up after each use.**

Natural Treatment for Diseases

The best options for controlling disease are purchasing of healthy plants and using careful plant management practices. Reading up on the growing habits and care of particular plants before buying them will alert the Plant Care Team to any potential difficulties. Certain plants are hardy in less than ideal environments. If the staff or residents want to try a more challenging plant, a reasonable amount of research before purchasing the plant will alert the Team to potential problems before they start.

As with the flu or common cold in humans, plant disease can spread quickly if not controlled. Occasionally, a diseased portion of a plant can be cut out, the wound dusted lightly with sulfur, and the plant isolated. This should be done away from people and animals, and only if discarding the plant is not possible. The Team must be aware that discarding a plant may be the best decision for other nearby plants.

By keeping water off foliage and flowers, keeping unhealthy, dead leaves and debris picked off and cleaned up, maintaining consistent watering procedures and air flow, and by following universal precautions, the chances of growing disease-free greenery are very good.

Seasonal Indoor Growing Conditions

All plants are affected by the changing seasons—even indoor plants. Flowering plants, plants that thrive in full sun, moisture-loving plants, plants that prefer shady conditions, and plants that set buds only when they've had a certain amount of light are a few examples. In some cases, the amount of light is the ingredient that increases or decreases plant growth. In other situations, the Home's heating and cooling system affects the plants' growth. During the course of the year, the Plant Care Team will see a variety of responses from plants where the "season is the reason" for changes.

These changes in plant growth can be encouraged or prevented if staff is aware of what to expect. The Home may want to consider refresher in-services for staff and residents. As the Plant Care Team carries out weekly plant care, they can consider the following factors and their effects on plants:

Long Days of Sunshine During Spring and Summer. In eastern, western, and southern windows: Is the sun shining directly on the plants? Are leaves filling out on trees and reducing sunlight?

Good effects: Plants come into bloom; overall growth increases; herbs grow stronger and fuller; seedlings grow well; soil stays warm; heat-loving plants do well; resident interest increases.

Undesirable effects or effects needing a plan: Sunburn on more sensitive plants; soil dries out faster; plants wilt even with moist soil; insects increase; certain plants need to be relocated for the season; residents dislike sitting in glare or "hot spots;" staff needs more time for plant care; possible need to install an awning or other means of shading; increased need for fertilizer; reduced light through windows due to outside leaf growth.

Air Conditioning: Is it blowing directly on plants or residents sitting near plants?

Good effects: Air circulation; cools leaves and soil; continued use of full-sun window exposure during hot months; prevents or reduces some insect and disease problems; comfort for residents.

Undesirable effects or effects needing a plan: Root rot and stem rot from cold soil; residents dislike sitting in a cool draft.

Short, Dark Days During Fall and Winter: Which windows are receiving the most unobstructed light?

Good effects: Plants can be moved back to southern and western windows during late fall and winter months; fertilizer and water needs and frequency decrease; importance of indoor plants and nature increases; poinsettias and other short-day bloom-setting plants bud; importance of artificial lights and associated activities increases; some windows may offer more light due to leaves falling from trees outside.

Undesirable effects or effects needing a plan: Slowing plant growth; some plants go dormant; overwatering can become a problem; residents may lose interest in window-grown plants; staff may need to purchase or ask for donations of light garden equipment; outside speakers and presentations may offer variety.

Heating (Forced Air or Baseboard): Is hot air blowing directly onto plants, or is heat rising from baseboard units below the plants?

Good effects: Soil, plants, and people stay warm and comfortable; evaporation takes place; heat-loving plants can grow here even in winter; air is circulating; soil is less likely to become soggy; water on leaves dries faster.

Undesirable effects or effects needing a plan: Soil dries faster; leaves may dry out; insects increase due to heat and dry conditions; staff may have to water more often.

Artificial Light for Year-Round Growing

As the days become shorter in late summer and early autumn, and the staff and residents start to mourn the passing of sunshine and warmth, the Plant Care Team can offer new growing opportunities and motivation with the assistance of fluorescent lights and growing shelves. A number of commercial grow-light units are on the market, or the staff may decide to construct their own. Donations from volunteer groups, and community or gardening association grants can also be considered during the planning process.

Commercial grow-light units may have one shelf (table model) with an attached fluorescent light unit, or two or three shelves with a light unit for each shelf. Some units come with automatic off-on timers and wheels for moving the unit from place to place. Other styles of light units have built-in planter boxes for soil and direct planting of seeds and/or plants.

A homemade light shelf can be constructed from sturdy, plastic, tubular snap-together shelves found at most discount stores. If mobility of the shelving is desired, the maintenance department can be consulted about adding wheels, or a unit with attached wheels may be considered. Some styles have adjustable shelves which can be raised and lowered, while others have a fixed distance between shelves. Flats or trays without drainage holes are placed on the shelves, and pots or flats with drainage holes are set into the larger trays. The surface area of the shelves should be compared with the size of the trays or flats to determine the best fit.

Artificial light tubes should be composed of one warm-white and one cool-white tube per fixture, should be long enough to cover the shelf from end-to-end, and will need to be left on for 12–14 hours per day for foliage houseplants. Blooming plants may need sixteen hours of light per day. Specialty flowering varieties such as orchids may grow better with specific grow light tubes. The lights will need to be positioned 6–12 inches above the plants or seedlings. The fixtures which hold the light tubes can be simple, utility types; chains can be attached to the ends to enable the fixtures to be raised and lowered to accommodate the height of the plants. The maintenance department will know how to rig the electrical connections to meet code requirements.

For ease of operation and the benefit of the plants, a timer can be attached to the light units to assure that they come on automatically in the morning and turn off late in the day. Investing in a reliable timer with a warranty will pay for itself in sturdy seedlings and healthy, blooming plants.

Some additional considerations for establishing a light garden:

- **Location:** Should be accessible to all residents; placed firmly to avoid tipping; lights will be on from early morning until later in the evening.

- **Size and number of shelves:** This will depend on the type and stage of plants: annual and vegetable seedlings grow quickly and require transplanting to larger pots; growing houseplants from seeds is a slower, smaller operation; exotic blooming plants may need more space.

- **Cost:** Will this be a retail purchase, donation, or a do-it-yourself project?

- **Ventilation:** Good airflow is required to prevent mold formation on plant leaves and to assist in drying the soil. A small fan can be positioned to blow above or below the foliage being careful to not blow directly on the leaves. If possible, situate the shelving away from any heating vents to prevent drying of the leaves.

- **Plant care:** Figure care of the grow-light plants into the Plant Care Team's schedule. Can some plants be assigned to residents? Additional attention is needed for watering (this may be a daily task as the seedlings grow) and transplanting.

- **Increased opportunities:** Growing annual flowers and vegetables from seed means that the residents and staff can choose the exact varieties they want. Unusual and blooming plants can be grown this way, and then used for interior decoration, gifts, prizes, special awards, and so forth.

- **A year-round growing plan** needs to be created to fully utilize the light unit.

- **Information gathering** related to the cultivation of individual plants will increase success, as will consultation with the community houseplant advisor.

- **Growing tips:** Rodale's *Encyclopedia of Indoor Gardening* suggests dusting the light tubes at least once a week for maximum light. Remember to replace tubes before the manufacturer's recommended expiration time (after about 80% of suggested use has gone by). Mark the installation date and the approximate date for the tube to be changed on the tube's end cap. Replace one bulb at a time to avoid causing light shock with the plants. For increased interest and learning opportunities, try a variety of foliage and blooming plants, seedlings, and cuttings.

- Purchase or find at the local library **a reliable and informative reference book on light gardening**. Use local resources such as a botanical garden and greenhouses for further information.

Growing and Propagating Houseplants

The majority of information about growing houseplants was covered in the *Care for indoor plants* section. Some additional tips for keeping houseplants happy and producing new plants are provided here.

The majority of houseplants need a warm environment to root. Additional heat from a commercial plant propagation mat is ideal but expensive. The top of a radiator may be useful, but too much heat may dry out the planting medium. Avoid cold drafts by placing cuttings in a plastic tent. Avoid cold surfaces by placing magazines or several layers of newspaper beneath the pots of propagating plants.

- **Use fertilizer with caution.** Fertilize during growing months only (early spring to early fall), using specific "houseplant" fertilizer, but using only **half** as much as the recommended amount **half** as often. Hold back on feeding plants from late autumn to early spring to allow plants to rest. During the short days of winter, plants manufacture food at a much slower rate. Consider using time-released fertilizer to reduce care time and eliminate the need for a fertilizer schedule. Don't use additional water-soluble fertilizers if you use a time-released fertilizer.

- **Only use clean pots.** All empty pots should be cleaned before planting. When green or crusty layers appear on the outside of pots with live plants, remove the plant and root ball, wrap it in damp newspaper, place it in a shady place and scrub the pot thoroughly. Wear waterproof gloves and scrub the pot with steel wool or a scouring pad, rinse well with water to remove particles, then soak the pots in a solution of ¾ cup chlorine bleach in one gallon of water for approximately thirty minutes. Allow the pots to dry completely, then repot the plant as soon as possible.

- **Rooting stem cuttings in water.** Any number of plants can be propagated this way including fibrous begonias, Persian shields, impatiens, aluminum plants, coleus, fittonia, and polka dot plants. Find a stem with a growing tip (where new leaves emerge at end of stem) and several sets of leaves growing along the stem. Using a sharp knife or scissors wiped off with alcohol, slice through the stem at the desired length (usually 4–6 inches from the growing tip), or cut the stem just below the fourth set of mature leaves. Remove the bottom set of leaves (may remove the next set if needed), and place the cutting in water and out of direct sunlight. Observe for root growth which usually takes two to four weeks.

- **Using rooting hormone** is another way to root a cutting. Dip the cut end of the stem in

---

Bleach Solution

to clean pots and containers

¾ cup   chlorine bleach
1 gallon   water

Wear waterproof gloves. Scrub pots with steel wool or a scouring pad to remove any buildup; rinse well with water to remove particles. Soak the pots in the bleach solution for approximately 30 minutes. Allow the pots to dry completely before reuse or repotting.

rooting powder (this can be purchased at garden centers), make a hole in moistened soil with a pencil (use a finely milled soil for seedlings), and place the cutting in the hole. Firm the soil around the stem and cover it with a plastic bag supported by a coat hanger frame or sticks. Set the pot out of direct sunlight to root. Roots usually form faster with rooting hormone. In two weeks, gently dig up one of the cuttings to check for roots and share your findings with the residents. If roots do not form, the cutting will wilt and eventually rot.

- **Leaf cuttings** can be fun and fascinating. Rex begonias, gloxinias, and streptocarpus plants can be multiplied by this method. Remove a healthy leaf, place it on a clean paper towel, turn it over, and with a very sharp knife or razor blade (wiped with alcohol), slice through the larger veins which branch from the main center vein of the leaf. Lightly dust the cuts with rooting hormone. Turn the leaf over, and place it on top of moist rooting medium (seedling soil). Pin down the leaf with clean, bent paper clips or hairpins, making sure the cuts on the leaf come in contact with the rooting medium. The ends of the paper clips or hairpins may pierce the leaf as they are inserted into the soil. Cover with a plastic bag supported with a bent coat hanger or sticks, and place in a warm spot out of direct sun. Keep the soil moist. Roots will form first, and then tiny plantlets will appear. Expect this to take at least three to four weeks. Check for roots by gently digging up one of the cuttings after three weeks. Transplant as needed.

- **Leaf stem rooting** can be done with African violets, fibrous begonias (the type with large, circular leaves) and other plants with long, well-formed leaf stems. Simply place the cut leaf stem in water or in a sterile rooting medium to root (rooting hormone may speed the process). To prevent shorter stemmed leaves from falling into the water, cover the top of the glass or jar with aluminum foil, make a slit in the foil, and insert the stem through the slit and into the water.

- **Rooting runners**: Spider plants and strawberry begonias (Saxifraga stolonifera), form "baby" plants on long stems which hang down around the pot. When large enough, these can simply be cut off and placed in water to root. Another way is to leave the runners connected, and place them in a pot of sterile soil next to the mother plant. Pin the plantlets down in the soil until they root, then trim away the runner. A plastic bag will help to keep the soil moist and the humidity high to encourage faster rooting.

- **For a challenge**, research cane cuttings, air layering, or try a variety of houseplants from seed.

- **Dividing offshoots and suckers**: This may be the easiest and fastest way to propagate, although the plant must produce these additions before they can be cut off. When a new plantlet is seen growing next to the mother plant, as is common with aloe vera, African violets, or bamboo palms, the entire plant can be carefully knocked out of the pot, and the new plant separated by slicing with a clean, sharp knife. Make sure that roots are attached to the new plant. Pot up the offshoot and treat as a new transplant, keeping the soil moist, the humidity high, and away from direct sun for at least a week.

- **Other methods**: Seeds provide a wide variety of choices for houseplants. Look for suppliers in the back of horticulture magazines. Some garden centers and most well-known mail-order catalogs carry a limited choice of houseplant seeds. Rhizomes from plants such as the rabbit's foot fern can be cut off and laid on top of the soil, then use the moist soil and plastic bag method to encourage rooting. See *References and resources* (p. 133) for recommended houseplant books which contain descriptions of propagation methods for a variety of plants.

Tips for Motivating Residents, Creating Spontaneity, and Covering Staffing Gaps

- Hold a *resident-centered* plant care session led by a volunteer professional from the community.

- Have special name tags or buttons for volunteer plant care residents.

- Make separate plant care schedules with eye-catching colors or pictures for resident volunteers.

- Arrange for a resident or a staff member to occasionally take photos of residents and Plant Care Team members at work.

- Have a few community volunteer backup people available (in addition to the Plant Care Team) to cover for illness, vacations, and other unexpected absences. Be sure to thoroughly orient them to the surroundings and procedures by having them accompany a regular Plant Person on his or her rounds.

- Invite the newspaper to do a story such as "Keeping Plants Green: Residents Garden Indoors at Fairworth Community."

Encouraging Residents to Care for Their Own Plants

The enthusiasm and interest of the Plant Care Team and the steps taken to include the residents in aspects of the growing indoor gardening environment will be the keys to motivating and enabling residents to participate in caring for their own houseplants. Some considerations:

- Invite all residents to participate in planning and preparing the indoor plant environment. Give them enough information to help them decide where and how they'd like to help out.

- Before asking residents about their interest in having a personal houseplant, be certain their room environment will support a plant successfully or can be altered to accommodate the plant. It is especially important to consider lighting needs and space.

- Approach each resident personally or hold a special session to ask the residents if they would like to have their own plant.

- Discuss how the Plant Care Team will assist the resident and what is expected of the resident. Respect the resident's right to refuse.

- If the resident's own room is not an appropriate houseplant environment, ask if he or she would like to take care of a plant in a public or sunroom area. Be sure to write the resident's name on the plant's tag.

- Provide choices for resident's plants. Have a book on hand with basic information about each kind of plant. This book should include common and scientific names, light and moisture needs, what country or type of climate it came from, eventual height, and other interesting information unique to each plant.

- Use plants currently in the resident's room when possible.

- If resident has a special request for a plant, research it and discuss it with the resident and Plant Care Team.

- Locate the plant in a resident's room where he or she can readily see and reach it.

- Discuss how special tools can be used by residents with limited strength.

- Discuss how residents with vision impairment can still enjoy plant care.

- Include family members in discussing plant choices if the resident is unable to choose or respond.

- Have a separate personal plant care schedule for participating residents.

- Encourage residents to participate in Garden Club meetings and other special discussions relating to houseplants.

- Consider allergies when choosing plants (e.g., blooming plants release pollen; some plants have irritating sap).

Learning to Be Spontaneous

Many spontaneous things will stimulate connections with the natural elements of the indoor growing environment. These spur-of-the-moment happenings keep residents alert to their green and growing surroundings and will keep them looking for more involvement. A combination of spontaneous discoveries and action plus scheduled events will gradually weave the awareness of nature and its benefits into the daily lives of the residents, staff, and visitors. Some specific approaches or things to try:

- Hold "Plant of the Week" discussions. Use residents' personal plants as topics. (Let participating residents know ahead of time.)

- Always have plants in various growing stages, and try various methods of propagation.

- Give residents a sense of usefulness and sharing by propagating from their personal plants.

- Point out new leaves, flowers, roots, sprouting seeds, and other horticultural events to residents and staff.

- Ask residents to report any suspicious signs of insects or diseases.

- Ask for resident volunteers to go on Plant Care rounds.

- Offer mini plant care sessions periodically to residents and staff.

- Post fliers announcing when seeds are sprouting, blooms are opening, herbs smell great, and Irma Smith's angel wing begonia cuttings are starting to grow roots.

- Bring in community experts to give mini talks about propagating plants, growing herbs, creating dish gardens, and other gardening topics.

- Offer houseplants grown by residents as prizes for "The 20th visitor to walk in the front door today," or "The last person in the cafeteria line for lunch."

- Involve residents in propagation and care of plants to be given as welcome gifts to newly admitted residents.

- Grow sensitive plants (*Mimosa pudica*) with residents for sharing with children.

- Take residents to see what other Neighborhoods in the Home are doing.

- Always have purchased, donated or library books available for reference and ideas.

- Ask an in-house or local occupational or recreation therapist to give a demonstration about using special tools or adapting tools for easier use by residents.

- Ask for resident input about purchasing an exotic plant from a catalog or local nursery.

- Hang a map of the world to mark countries from which residents' plants and others in the Neighborhood originate. The map should be hung at resident eye-level.

- Create easy access to view outside gardens, trees, bird feeders, and landscaping.

- Keep items handy such as garden dweller hand puppets (e.g., spider, ladybug, bat, frog), gardening books, and games for use by staff, visitors, and residents.

On-the-Spot Things to Do with Families and Visitors

Everyone who visits a nursing home or other residential care facility needs to be included in the opportunity to care for the indoor growing environment. The Plant Team can help to make this possible in several creative ways. Consider the following suggestions:

- Have the Neighborhood calendar accessible to all visitors; include residents' personal plant care scheduled times on it.

- Arrange a potting table with basic tools, soil, and containers with appropriate signage inviting visitors to exercise their green thumbs. Post a list of plant care tasks that anyone can do such as picking off dead leaves, dusting with feather duster and plain water, or for the more skilled novice, transplanting designated plants. Include a request to return tools and equipment when finished.

- Provide a reference guide for looking up information about plants and bookmark pages about plants found in the Neighborhood.

- Encourage everyone to rub and smell the fragrant herbs.

- Invent or purchase a garden game and keep it available.

- Ask a community garden or civic club to donate children's gardening books.

- Have materials available to make a seed collage. Donated and outdated seed packets or bulk seeds from garden centers are ideal for artwork. Use nontoxic, untreated seeds. Large seeds such as sunflowers and pumpkin work best. Offer construction paper, glue and a sample of a finished collage.

- Suggest cutting out magazine pictures to add to the giant garden collage in progress. (Borrow scissors from nurses' station or other staff and return when finished).

- Suggest visiting other Neighborhoods in the home to see their greenery and indoor garden projects.

- Make a Concentration houseplant card game. Use photos cut from identical but inexpensive houseplant books or magazines or good catalogs. Used bookstores can be a good source for these items.

Involving the Confused Resident and the Resident with Limited Response

The comfort of companionship and the stimulation of the senses experienced by the resident and the staff person (or volunteer) as they work together are the most important aspects of this kind of interaction. The completion of a project or the production of a finished item is of little importance.

Before involving a confused resident in gardening activities, it's helpful for the staff member to have information about the resident's prior gardening interests. People with memory loss are more easily involved in activities that were familiar to them at one time. How this information is obtained will depend on who conducts the indoor/outdoor activities, the process decided on by the Plant or Neighborhood Committee, and the Home's policies. It may also be helpful to ask family members to share background about the resident's past preferences.

Have materials ready prior to inviting the resident(s) to participate. Give verbal directions one at a time, and use physical demonstration. Sometimes the recognition of the task will motivate the resident to try, and automatic memory of past experiences will enable him or her to do the task without instruction. Stay with the resident, offer encouragement and praise, or redirect the resident if he or she becomes confused or frustrated.

Any activity or interaction involving food or handling plants should be conducted with prior knowledge of a resident's **allergies and dietary restrictions**.

When gardening with residents who are confused, use the following suggested guidelines:

- For weekly Garden Club meetings, wear a uniform that clearly illustrates the activity. For example, a straw hat with flowers, an apron with gardening tools painted on it, or a smock with large, colorful flowers. Wearing garden gloves for at least part of the interaction may also be helpful.

- Use an eye-catching, recognizable item (e.g., a hand puppet to introduce the plant or garden topic). Clever, larger-than-life puppets of ladybugs, bats, spiders, and other garden dwellers are soft, cute, and can bring out the residents' senses of humor. Look for these in better toy or variety stores. Keep these items available in the same location for use by all staff during spontaneous interactions.

- Simplify the activity—keep it short and sweet.

- Consider the senses: smelling, seeing, feeling/touching, tasting, hearing, laughing/humor.

- Choose only nontoxic plants for direct contact with confused residents.

- Give the resident two clear choices when-ever possible.

- Use tools with blunt edges and easy-to-hold handles. Colorful tools may be helpful as well.

- Work with small groups (4 at the most), or do the same short interaction one-on-one.

- Read up on heirloom houseplants and flow-ers such as the cast iron plants, parlor palms, lilacs, and pansies. Discuss old-fashioned home remedies such as mustard plasters and mint tea. Make recipes using produce and herbs from the residents' garden.

- Use phrases and terms such as "the back forty," "the parlor" (where houseplants were kept), "planting by the moon," and "The Farmer's Almanac."

- Find opportunities to use residents' names in large, clear print (e.g., on plants, photo-graphs, as part of a garden collage, on large calendars).

- Consider the enjoyment of the person con-ducting the activity. Choose topics appro-priate for the residents, yet stimulating to the presenter as well.

- Plan the sessions with 2 or 3 of the follow-ing topics: herb of the month; herb-flavored snack; houseplant, tree, and/or flower of the month; houseplant care; flower arranging; seasonal poetry and stories; texture of the month; insect and backyard wildlife of the month; gardening tools and equipment; gar-den themes, environmental songs, and music.

For more activity ideas and spontaneous topics, see *The Gardening Calendar* (pp. 99–130).

Green Spaces for Residents

Where do residents traditionally gather between planned activities or events? Are they found in the dining room, sitting at their usual table, waiting for the next meal which might be hours away? Do they stay in their rooms reading, watching tele-vision, or napping? Are they seen sitting in front of a large window staring at the outdoor scenery?

The creation of an indoor plant and garden environment provides residents and visitors with appealing, attractive locations for gathering and visiting, and it offers built-in reasons for seeking out these places. Green spaces are best located near a good light source such as a wall of windows, a sunporch, or a light cart filled with plants. The residents will seek out these locations to enjoy a sense of comfort and serenity, or to participate in stimulating visual and hands-on activity.

The important characteristics of these spaces, whether large or small, are the equally compatible atmosphere for people and plants, comfortable seating, space to maneuver wheelchairs and walk-ers, safe pathways, and interesting views of out-door settings. Chances are, the Home will have several locations where small pockets of greenery can be combined with seating arrangements for two or three people, and larger areas to accommo-date several family members and friends.

Each neighborhood team will need to exam-ine the possibilities for creating green spaces in their neighborhood. "Green space appeal" can be considered using the following guidelines:

- Accessibility to residents and safe features such as sturdy chairs for ambulatory resi-dents, within sight of staff if help is needed

- Companion animals' safety

- Adequate visitor seating

- Items or activities to occupy and entertain children

- Temperature and lighting (may be artificial) which is equally adequate for people and plants

- A diverse display of greenery such as hang-ing baskets, table plants, and/or floor plants

- Various stages of plant growth and types of propagation (e.g., seedlings, stem cut-tings, root cuttings)

- A variety of plants (e.g., flowering, heir-loom, exotic, fragrant, textured, fruiting)

- Plant name labels in each pot and additional information about the culture and origin of the plants posted on a bulletin board or placed on a table

- A sense of privacy or screening provided by leaves and branches of large plants

- Seasonal window views with landscape shrubs that provide interesting branch formations or dried foliage such as grasses; bird feeders, baths, and bird houses; wreaths decorated with bird food; a children's natural playground; a pond or other water feature; blooming shrubs; spring through fall floral blooms in many colors; variegated and unusual foliage

- The soothing sound of water from a small fountain or indoor water feature

- Chirping birds

- Resident volunteers for plant care

- Ease of maintenance

- Have residents choose names for green spaces (e.g., Sunrise Garden, Herb Corner, The Jungle)

Getting Green with Children

The Gardening Calendar offers suggestions for seasonal activities with children and residents. Step-by-step instructions will be provided where needed. Review *Intergenerational activities* (pp. 26–27) and keep these additional points in mind:

- When handling plants or serving food, be sure that children and residents aren't allergic to them.

- Use safety precautions and universal precautions.

- Find volunteers who are good with children.

- Call the local newspaper when a colorful, photogenic event is to be held.

Garden Group Ideas

Encouraging residents to make their own choices about the Garden Club agenda is the main issue. This may take some prompting by the staff, but should result in higher resident satisfaction. Encourage the group to choose a name for itself.

The most enjoyable and easiest way to plan Garden Club meetings is to consider the natural events of each season. The groups may decide to have one project or topic at each meeting, or to have a project continue over two or three meetings. During the winter months the topics may revolve around indoor plants, then begin to focus on outdoor plants as spring approaches. The members may prefer to have different categories of activities for each meeting such as "Houseplant of the Week," "Weekly Garden Book Excerpt," "How to Start New Plants," and so forth. The monthly calendars will list timely ideas for indoor and outdoor gardening topics.

Using Fragrant Herbs, Oils and Substances

Fragrances, both pleasant and unpleasant, can be a very powerful tool for resident interaction. Certain aromas can be used for reminiscing, stimulating conversation, and whetting the appetite. Others result in a calming effect, while some fragrances will perk up a lethargic person.

Many useful aromas are available through fresh herbs, flowers, and other natural materials. These are safe, inexpensive, and easy to grow. Also consider foods, herbs, spices, household articles, food flavorings, and additional pleasant (or stinky) sources for sensory stimulation. Here are a few:

- Fresh toast or bread

- Cooked cabbage

- Apple pie

- Dried or fresh chives, sage, cinnamon, cloves, pepper

- A well-worn sock; line-dried pillowcase; wet wool; Ivory or Fels Naptha bar soap; toothpaste

- Peppermint, licorice, almond flavorings

- Rosemary, roses, marigolds, and lavender

- Aged compost

- Freshly cut grass

- Strawberries

The discipline of using single oils or combinations of aromatic or essential oils derived from plants to bring about a specific reaction is known professionally as *aromatherapy*. **In the hands of a trained and educated individual**, aromatherapy can be beneficial and effective.

For the purposes of the Plant Care Team and others interacting with residents, it is recommended that before using any so-called "essential oils" or aromatherapy materials, the following factors are considered:

- Any facility policy applying to staff for using what may be considered "alternative treatment approaches"

- Potential allergic responses in residents and staff

- The use and high concentration of **true essential oils** may include risks. Specific ones can cause burning of eyes or skin. Some should be avoided during pregnancy. Some are fatal if swallowed. Certain oils can be stimulating while others can produce a sedative effect.

- The quality and composition of aromatic oils

- The purpose for which oils or fragrant materials are intended

- The approval of the Home's medical director

- Consultation with a qualified aromatherapist

- Cost of purchasing quality oils

- Benefit as compared with traditional medical approach

- Benefit of training in aromatherapy

Plants for Animals

Certain plants can be grown for the amusement of pets, to distract them from chewing on the potentially toxic houseplants, or for snacks. Before offering any homegrown plant material as food for an animal, a veterinarian or other knowledgeable expert should be consulted.

A cat in a nursing home setting can usually find plenty of things to keep it amused and occupied. Occasional boredom or just curiosity may lead a kitty to nibbling on houseplants. Growing small pots of the herb catnip, or wheat, oat, and rye grasses may prevent cats from grazing on other houseplants. Growing these plants will also provide a fun and useful intergenerational activity.

Catnip or catmint (*Nepeta cataria*) is enjoyed fresh or dried by feline residents. Anyone who has witnessed the results of a cat–catnip combination will agree that both cats and people enjoy the amusement. The biologically active compound nepetalactone causes behavior changes in approximately two-thirds of adult cats who eat it. Rolling, scooting, rubbing, and leaping are a few of the laughable antics produced from smelling and ingesting the leaves. These effects are harmless, and cats will self-regulate their use of the herb. The **dried** leaves may produce the most amusing reaction. Some cats may eat the **fresh** leaves with pleasure but not show any behavior change.

The *Rodale Herb Book* advises to start catnip from seed in the garden, and to avoid bruising the seedlings. If the leaves become damaged, the escaping oil will bring more cats to the garden than any home could want. When it's time to harvest, cut sprigs from the plant, and remove the individual leaves after going indoors. To dry the leaves, cut lengths of stems, bring inside, and hang in a ventilated place out of direct sunlight. When the leaves are crispy, strip them off, crush them, and place them in a cheesecloth, panty hose, or net bag with the opening firmly tied closed. Pinch the bag to release the aroma, give it to the cat, and watch the fun.

Grasses are not as appealing to cats, but can be attractive in their own right, are inexpensive to grow, and can be trimmed or thrown out when they become too leggy. Grasses need at least six hours of sun, or 10–12 hours of artificial light to grow well.

Rabbits, guinea pigs, hamsters, and birds also have needs and preferences for fresh greens. Caution must be taken to offer these items in proper amounts and under controlled conditions with staff monitoring. Check with a veterinarian or animal expert before giving any fresh greens to pets.

Part 3: Nurturing and Keeping the Growing Spirit

Community, Family, and Professional Support

As the indoor garden environment has developed through planning and implementation, the Plant Committee Chair(s) will have realized the tremendous advantage in recruiting volunteer experts. The difficulty in attracting these valuable people and in keeping them interested enough to stay with the Committee will become apparent.

What can the Committee Chair(s) do to maintain the continuity of the local community and staff membership? The following guidelines will suggest ways to keep good members and to motivate those lagging members whose interest seems to have fizzled.

- Read, understand, and use the Home's mission statement and other guidelines recommended by the administration for committee formation and staff nurturing and empowerment.

- Periodically review the Committee's initial plan of action for indoor and outdoor garden implementation and strive to follow it within reason.

- Have clearly written agendas for each Plant Committee meeting.

- Include each member in opportunities for contributing concerns, comments, and topics for the next meeting.

- Recognize each committee member as a participating individual, remembering to empower the frontline staff to carry out their committee assignments.

- Give equal consideration to everyone's suggestions.

- Report evidence of the benefits of human interaction with plants and gardens (e.g., "Studies show that…"). Compile a notebook of informal (anecdotal) observations of residents and their positive interaction with the plants and gardens as reported by the Plant Team, staff and volunteers.

- Serve refreshments!

- Praise and graciously thank those who make the effort to attend and participate.

- Budget for inexpensive but nice spontaneous rewards for attendance (e.g., bookmarks, candy bars, packets of seeds, starter plants, other small gifts).

- Track volunteer tasks and hours. Plan and implement appropriate recognition.

- Budget for continuing education, special in-services, and/or educational trips for Plant Committee members and Plant Care Teams.

Recordkeeping

Every organized gardener keeps a journal of his or her accomplishments. A brief description of what has been done each year enables the gardener to build on experience, to repeat successes, or correct mistakes. This applies to indoor greenery as well as outdoor gardens. A log of weekly indoor plant care can assist the Plant Care Team to remember when certain tasks such as fertilizing and taking cuttings were done. A sense of shared responsibility and respect for good management is produced when a Team member or a resident gardener can look in the log and say, "We planted those sensitive seeds on March 7, and they germinated in just seven days." Confusion is avoided when a relief Team member checks the log and sees that all plants in the West window were fertilized the previous Tuesday. A sturdy, waterproof three-ring binder can hold the information securely.

The Plant Care Log serves to guide the Plant Care Team and the volunteers in each Neighborhood in the following ways:

- Provides guidelines for routine plant care.

- Describes additional or specialized care for specific varieties of plants found in that Neighborhood.

- Contains weekly plant care sheets.

- Includes descriptions of insect, disease problems and treatment, or where to find a reference about them.

- Describes various ways to propagate houseplants (with a reference books available).

- Lists names of community experts to call for advice.

- Contains community volunteers' sign-in and hours worked sheets.

- Contains Plant Care Team's schedule.

- Includes reminders of safety precautions and personnel to contact in case of emergency.

Figure 4 is an example of a weekly plant care form that can be included in the Plant Log; a blank version for copying is located in the appendix. The checklist titled *Caring for the indoor plants* (starts on p. 39) can also be copied and included in the log for referring to the steps of routine plant care and recognition of insects and disease problems.

Building a Reference Library

Having reliable references on hand when needed is a must for building confidence and credibility. An inexpensive but informative library can be created in several ways. The following resources are suggested:

- Used book stores

- Donations from families, garden clubs, civic groups

- Library book sales

- Garage sales

- Memorial donations of books or funds from family members

- Internet web sites (the best are university-related)

Turning Dreams into Reality

The Plant Committee can review their initial brainstorming wish list and compare this with its present needs. With several months of experience under their belts, the members and individual Plant Care Teams will have realized their actual needs, and be able to more accurately propose their wishes for the future, and streamline their own organization. A general checklist to review might look like this:

❏ Do residents have adequate space or display methods for their personal plants?

❏ Are residents being encouraged to participate in the indoor gardening activities and are they being recognized for their efforts?

❏ Are appropriate gardening tools and equipment available for use by residents and staff?

❏ Is more fluorescent lighting needed in the hallways or green spaces to support the plants' health and growth?

❏ Have matching plant containers and pots been purchased?

❏ Do volunteers play a consistent role and are they being recognized for their efforts?

❏ Have green spaces been created?

❏ Have funding sources been utilized and civic clubs attracted to the indoor gardening effort?

WEEKLY INDOOR PLANT CARE NOTES

LOCATION: Greenfield Hall next to room #1218

PLANTS: (1) Lady palm (floor plant)

(2) Beefsteak plant (on table)

(3) Wax plant (on plant stand)

(4) African violet (on table; see "Special Care" section in log)

DATE & PERSON	ROUTINE CARE	FERTILIZED	COMMENTS
8/9/02 S. Smith	√	8/9/02	*Some spider mites on beefsteak; sprayed with Safer's*
8/26/02 S. Smith	√		*Not as many spider mites; sprayed again*

Figure 4   Indoor Plant Care Log Sample

The OUTSIDE STORY....

Phase III
Outdoor Gardening

Part 1: Preparation

Assessment of Existing Outdoor Gardening Areas

Many Homes already have some form of outdoor gardening environment in place. Some may even be using the Eden Alternative concept. These guideline questions are similar to the ones in *Phase I, How Green Are We?* for the outdoor gardens (p. 3). Consider the following points:

- Are resident gardens in place? Where, in relation to the building are the beds located?

- Are the garden plots accessible to residents who are ambulatory and/or in wheelchairs?

- Are the exit doors automated? Can the residents operate them?

- Are some of the beds raised for use by residents in wheelchairs and those who have trouble stooping or bending over?

- What equipment and tools are available? What equipment or tools need to be obtained, borrowed or rented?

- How is water obtained?

- Who on staff cares for the garden? Is separate time allowed within the employees' shift? Have these behind-the-scenes gardeners been invited to join the Plant Committee?

- Is gardening included in the residents' scheduled activities?

- Have staff members received any additional training in gardening methods?

- What gardening books and resources are available for staff reference?

- Are organic gardening methods practiced?

- Is information available about toxic plants?

- Are volunteers involved? Are community resources used?

- Is gardening an itemized part of the budget?

Outdoor Gardening Committee Members

Staff and volunteers caring for the outdoor gardens will most likely be the same people who have been involved with the indoor greenery. If the outdoor gardeners are different from the indoor Plant Care Team, it's important that they are informed about the general actions and functions of the Plant Committee.

As with the indoor plant care, the people responsible for outdoor gardening will need guidelines for garden maintenance and resident interaction. Inclusion of a gardener on the committee who is well-acquainted with **organic gardening** is recommended. An in-service presentation by a professional from a local university or organic gardening association can provide up-to-date information and guidance. Policies for use of chemical herbicides and pesticides must be carefully discussed, and the potentially toxic consequences for residents, animals, wildlife, and all persons must be understood.

Special Training Offers and Provisions

The combined expertise of staff, residents, and volunteers will produce a wealth of gardening knowledge. It is important to keep these participants informed of current gardening approaches and trends. The local Cooperative Extension Service, garden associations, botanical gardens, and universities can supply updated information, and will increase the community contacts needed by the Plant and Garden Teams. The Plant Committee Chair can research these opportunities or appoint a Community Relations committee member to track them down.

How to Involve the Residents in the Gardening Experience

The participation of the residents in the implementation of the outdoor gardens depends largely on including them in the planning phase. Invite the residents and their families to attend and participate in scheduled planning meetings about the outdoor gardens. The Plant Committee can decide how to best design and distribute the invitations. Use the talents of a local graphic designer or computer guru (i.e., staff, resident, or volunteer) to create attractive and appealing fliers, which might include old-fashioned or reminiscent drawings or photos.

At the meeting, a short history of the existing gardens can be explained along with a basic plan of action for the future. Resident participation in gardening activities can be explained and encouraged as it relates to overall well-being. A short explanation of the benefits of gardening might include increased socialization, the opportunity for physical exercise, the anticipation of growth and change, a sense of accomplishment, and the revival of pleasant and familiar memories. Make it clear that resident and family input is greatly needed to

create a sense of home, and continue the opportunity for the residents to enjoy outdoor gardening in a personally meaningful way. Suggestions gained from this meeting can then be applied to a more specific plan of action for year-round gardening activities.

Children, Animals and Elders in the Garden

Preparation paves the way for awareness of certain considerations and precautions when bringing together the variety of living beings in a residential setting. As interactions are planned, the expertise of child daycare and schoolteachers, animal and wildlife experts, community gardening enthusiasts, and local professional resources will combine with the skills of the staff, residents, and volunteers at the Home. The Plant Committee Chair will benefit from a well-informed core of committee members who are able to share the diverse responsibilities and activities of the gardening adventure.

Brainstorming for Ideas and Dreams of Future Garden Development

Making the best of what is available is a practical place to begin. As the garden grows and the gardeners' experience grows, however, the desire for better, more efficient, and more accessible ways to enjoy gardening will become evident. Continuing community outreach will fire the imagination of civic groups or individuals wanting to contribute to the progress of this life-giving opportunity.

What are some of the dreams for assisting the gardeners and improving the gardens? Take time to carefully consider improvements, talk with residents and families, ask volunteers and visitors, and make a list. A sample list might include:

- Automatic doors to the garden that residents can use
- Appropriately enclosed garden area for residents with dementia with attractive, low-maintenance fencing
- Blacktop pathways and appropriately edged ground beds for walking and wheelchair safety

- Comfortable tools for everyone
- Low-maintenance raised beds
- A resident-oriented gazebo or shaded porch
- More garden books
- The ability to purchase annuals, herbs and perennial plants, seeds, and start-up supplies
- A state-of-the-art watering system including watering wands, hoses, a hose caddy and lightweight hose for use by the residents
- A cold frame with an automatic lid opener
- Birdbaths, wildlife feeders, and birdhouses
- A potting bench
- A lightweight, well-balanced wheelbarrow
- A state-of-the-art tiller
- Well-built compost bins made of durable material (e.g., synthetic lumber)
- Wildlife attracting plants and shrubs
- A garden shed
- A bread machine
- A food dehydrator
- Garden statuary
- The sky's the limit!

Part 2: Beginning to Grow

Taking a *Good* Look at Existing Garden Resources

The Eden Alternative guidelines recommend that "outdoor gardens should add to rather than replace indoor plants." Try to get comfortable with caring for the indoor plants before breaking ground for, or enlarging the outdoor beds. Keep in mind that planting a small but successful outside garden will be more rewarding than a large one that goes to weeds.

If gardening activities are already in place, the Plant Committee Chair can examine the outdoor plots and ask questions about last year's crops if she or he was not participating at that time. If appropriate, invite an alert resident to assist in the assessment. Take notes and draw simple diagrams of the area. Regardless of the season, the following items can be considered:

General Concerns

Accessibility

- Are the exit doors automatic?

- Is there a level, shaded area for seats and wheelchairs?

- Are there any safety issues such as uneven ground, especially along the edge of the ground-level beds? cracks and gaps in sidewalks?

Equipment, Resources, and Staff

- What equipment and tools are available? What needs to be obtained, borrowed, or rented?

- Where is the water source? Is the hose long enough to reach all areas?

- Is there a compost pile? a cold frame?

- Who on staff cares for the garden? Is separate time allowed within the employees' shift?

- Have these behind-the scenes gardeners been invited to join the Plant Committee?

- Is gardening included in the scheduled activities?

Location Considerations

- Is the area secured by fencing? Is traffic a concern?

- Are there any concerns about the surrounding neighborhood's activities?

- Are there stands of poison ivy or other potentially toxic plants that should be removed or relocated?

- Are there stinging insect nests, such as wasps or yellow jackets, present or forming in the gardening area?

Safety Issues

Safety is always of prime concern. Discuss how preventative measures can be taken to guard against cuts, scrapes, falls, and toxic exposure involving all that participate.

Interest in the garden will be an ongoing event, with residents wanting to go outside in the cool of the evening or on weekends to weed, water, or pick flowers and vegetables. Is it possible for them to get to the garden on their own if they use wheelchairs or walkers? If the doors to the garden are not automated, are evening and weekend staff encouraged to assist residents who want to garden? How are these staff members included in the safety education process?

Consider the following measures and include safety in the gardening policies:

- Be aware of **resident allergies** including food and insects. Discuss the same with **schoolteachers** before intergenerational activities begin.

- Have a standard policy about **residents and outdoor temperatures**.

- Observe standard policy about **first aid**.

- Always **monitor residents who are confused** when using tools or plant materials.

- Mark tool handles with bright yellow and black paint or tape.

- Know which tools are in use and collect them when finished.

- **Never** leave a tool laying in a path or on a seat.

- Use garden gloves as needed.

- Water when the least number of people are around and alert them about the hose.

- Keep tools rust-free.

- Secure all tools when not in use with exception of basic tools left available for after-hours resident and family use.

- Select **nontoxic plants**. Consider residents, visitors, domestic animals, and birds when choosing plants.

- Use **only organic, nontoxic sprays or dusts**.

- Prune overhanging branches.

- Consider a brief educational in-service about this list with the title and corresponding posters "Gardening Safety is a Natural."

Toxic Outdoor Garden Plants to Avoid

Consideration for residents, children and animals must be given during participation in gardening activities and on a daily basis. If there are toxic plants already present in the garden beds, discuss how to relocate or dispose of these plants. The safest approach is to start with plants that have been identified by a knowledgeable person, then proceed by choosing the least toxic varieties. Safety measures should be taken if the plant cannot be identified (e.g., fence it in, cut it back to the ground, pull it up).

General guidelines for selecting safe plants recommend caution when considering any of the following:

- Any plant not identified by a knowledgeable person.

- Plants that produce berries other than familiar edible fruits like raspberries, blueberries, or strawberries.

- Any form of lily. Although some may be harmless, many lily bulbs are toxic to animals.

- Plants with thorns or prickles.

- Any plant in the morning glory family.

- Any form of ivy.

- Any plant that produces a *spathe* or leaf-like part, often decorative, and contains an elongated protrusion. Examples of these are the peace lily (*Spathyphyllum*), *Anthurium*, and jack-in-the-pulpit.

- Any plant grown from a bulb (with the exception of begonias grown from a corm).

- Any plant reported to have been used as a mind- or mood-altering agent.

- "Weeds." Some are considered noxious (i.e., harmful to the health) even though they are commonly seen and often visually appealing. Examples include jimson weed, nightshade, and poison hemlock.

- Leaves from trees that produce fruit with pits or seeds (e.g., apricot, peach, pear, plum, nectarine).

- Fruit pits and seeds.

- Nuts from trees in the wild.

- Plants that produce sticky sap. These saps can cause allergic dermatitis.

If an adult or child is suspected of ingesting a toxic plant, remove any portion of plant left in his or her mouth and call your Poison Control Center. Locate the phone number for your local Poison Control hotline, or call the American Association of Poison Control Centers at 1–800–222–1222. Prepare for plant poisoning emergencies by having your local hotline number posted at every phone and write it in the following box and the inside back cover for future reference:

IN CASE OF PLANT POISONING EMERGENCY, CALL:

Table 3 (pp. 64–67) contains plants considered **very toxic** to humans and/or companion animals such as cats, dogs, and rabbits. These plants can produce symptoms affecting the digestive and/or nervous system, and, in some cases, severe dermatitis. The severity of the symptoms depend on the species of plant, and the age, health and weight of the individual who ingests the plant, the amount of foliage or number of berries ingested, and the toxicity of the plant. **In some cases just one or two leaves or berries can be fatal.**

This list is by no means a comprehensive list. Many additional plants cause mild to moderate toxic symptoms. It is essential that each Plant Committee examine their own **local toxic plant lists** available through their local Poison Control Center and/or university with a department of horticulture.

Examining Existing Garden Beds

- Are green plants visible now?
- Approximately how many hours of sunlight per day does each bed get?

Ground-level Beds

- Has the soil in the ground-level beds been turned?
- Are there any soggy areas?

After the above evaluation, information can be shared with the Plant Committee or the individual Neighborhood caring for the garden area. The following planning questions can then be asked:

- Should the same amount of ground be planted this year?
- Are raised beds needed? Would large plastic containers or pots be sufficient until further arrangements can be made?
- How many residents are able and willing to participate in the gardening process?
- Are there volunteers available from the staff and/or community groups?
- How much time will be given to staff to maintain the garden?
- Consider that flowers, vegetables, herbs, fruit, and wildlife as well as residents, children, and staff eventually will be growing together in the garden.
- Who is going to be the backup staff gardener(s)?
- Does the Home use contractors for maintaining the landscape? If so, invite them to become a part of the outdoor gardening program. Communicate with landscaping contractors about where garden beds and plants are being located to keep them from accidentally removing new plantings while weeding. Also, do these contractors practice organic gardening techniques? If not, will the use of chemicals pose a hazard to residents, companion animals, or visitors?
- What additional training is available or needed for staff gardeners?
- Are gardening books available?
- Discuss any other needs, dreams, or wishes of residents and staff. Set some approximate time frames to reach these goals.

Raised Beds

- Examine the existing raised beds. Is their construction strong? Is the wood in good condition? Are the support legs sturdy and in good repair? Are there any sharp edges or splinters that may pose a hazard?
- Try sitting in a wheelchair to work in the raised beds. Is the soil loose and easy to

Table 3   Some Toxic Outdoor Plants

COMMON NAME	SCIENTIFIC NAME	TOXICITY NOTES
Aconite, Monkshood	Aconitum varieties	
African lily, Lily of the Nile	Agapanthus	
Allium, ornamental onion (many varieties)	Allium	Concern for animals
Aloe, Burn plant	Aloe vera	Concern for animals
Amaranth	Celosia cristata	Concern for animals
Amaryllis	Hipeastrum	
Angel's trumpet	Brugmansia	
Apple tree (leaves and pits; especially when wilted)	Malus varieties	
Apricot (leaves and pits)	Prunus	
Autumn crocus	Colchicum autumnale	
Avocado	Persea americana	Concern for animals
Azalea (wild and cultivated, varieties depend on geographical locale)	Rhododendron varieties	
Baby's breath (dried or cut florist flower)	Gypsophila varieties	Potentially harmful to animals
Baneberry (red and white; also called White cohosh)	Actaea	
Bittersweet	Celastrus scandens	
Black acacia	Robinia pseudoacacia	
Black cherry (leaves and pits)	Prunus	
Black henbane	Hyoscyamus niger	
Black locust	Robinia pseudoacacia	
Black nightshade, Climbing nightshade	Solanum dulcamara	
Bleeding heart	Dicentra species	
Buckeye (nut)	Aesculus parviflora	
Bushman's poison, Wintersweet	Acokanthera species	
Cardinal flower	Lobelia cardinalis	
Carolina jessamine or jasmine	Gelsemium sempervirens	
Castor bean	Ricinus communis	
Cedar, white	Thuja occidentalis	
Century plant	Agave americana	
Cestrum, night-scented Jessamine (jasmine), and other varieties	Cestrum nocturnum, C. elegans, C. 'Newellii'	
Chenille plant	Acalypha hispida	Concern for animals
Cherry (leaves and pits; including choke-cherry, black cherry, cherry laurel, and other varieties)	Prunus varieties	Concern for animals and people
Chinaberry (fruit with pits)	Melia azedarach	
Chinese lantern	Physalis angulata	
Chinese tallow tree	Sapium sebiferum	
Chives, Wild onions	Allium species	
Christmas rose, Lenten rose	Helleborus	
Clematis	Clematis	
Clivia, Kaffir lily	Clivia miniata	
Coral tree	Erythrina	
Crabapple (leaves and seeds; especially when wilted)	Malus	
Creeping Charlie	Glechoma hederacea	

Table 3   Some Toxic Outdoor Plants (continued)

COMMON NAME	SCIENTIFIC NAME	TOXICITY NOTES
Crocus, autumn	Colchicum autumnale	
Crown vetch	Coronilla varia	
Cyclamen	Cyclamen	
Daffodil (bulb)	Narcissus species	Minor concern for people; concern for animals
Daphne	Daphne varieties	
Death camus, Black snakeroot	Zigadanus varieties	
Delphinium (many varieties)	Delphinium species	
Dusty Miller (see botanical name to differentiate from Dusty Miller/ Cinararia)	Senecio viravira	
Elderberry	Sambucus varieties	Minor concern for people; concern for animals
Euonymous	Euonymous	
Euphorbia	Euphorbia species	Minor concern for people; concern for animals
Flax	Linum usitatissimum	Concern for animals
Flowering tobacco, tree tobacco, cultivated tobacco	Nicotiana glauca, N. tabacum	
Foxglove	Digitalis purpurea	
Fritillary, snakeshead, checker lily	Fritillaria meleagris	
Ginkgo biloba	Ginkgo biloba	
Golden chain tree	Laburnum anagyroides	
Heavenly bamboo	Nandina domestica	Concern for animals
Heliotrope	Heliotropum arborenscens	
Hellebore, Christmas rose, Lenten rose	Helleborus species	
Hemlock, poison	Conium maculatum	
Hemlock, water	Cicuta species	
Henbane, Black henbane	Hyoscyamus niger	
Holly (many varieties with berries)	Ilex species	
Hyacinth	Hyacinthus orientalis	
Iris, blue flag	Iris species	Minor concern for people; concern for animals
Jequirity bean	Arbus precatorius	
Jerusalem cherry	Solanum pseudocapsicum	
Jessamine, night-scented	Cestrum	
Jessamine, Carolina, Yellow	Gelsimium sempervirens	
Jimson weed, thorn apple	Datura stramonium	
Juniper	Juniperus species	Minor concern for people; concern for animals
Lantana	Lantana camara	
Larkspur	Delphinium species	
Lily, checkered	Fritillaria meleagris	

Table 3   Some Toxic Outdoor Plants (continued)

COMMON NAME	SCIENTIFIC NAME	TOXICITY NOTES
Lily, glory or climbing	Gloriosa superba	
Lily of the valley	Convallaria majalis	
Lobelia, Cardinal flower, Indian pink	Lobelia inflata	
Lily-of-the-valley bush, mountain pieris	Pieris japonica	
Locust, black and yellow (seeds)	Robinia pseudoacacia	
Loquat	Eriobotyra japonica	
Love-in-a-mist	Nigella damascena	
Love-lies-bleeding	Amaranthus caudatus	
Lupine	Lupinus	
May apple	Podophyllum peltatum	
Mistletoe, American and European	Phloradendron flavescens, Viscum album	
Monkshood	Aconitum species	
Moon flower seeds	Ipomoea species	
Moonseed, yellow parilla (wild vine)	Menispermum	
Morning glory seeds	Ipomoea species	
Mountain laurel	Kalmia latifolia, K. angustifolia	
Mushrooms	All species	**Can be fatal.** Avoid all types found growing in the wild unless evaluated by an expert.
Nandina	Nandina domestica	
Narcissus	Narcissus species	
Nightshade, black and common	Solanum nigra, S. americana	
Nightshade, bittersweet and climbing	Solanum dulcamara	
Oleander	Nerium oleander	
Pieris, lily-of-the-valley bush, mountain fetterbush	Pieris japonica, P. floribunda	
Pine tree	Pinus	Concern for animals
Pittosporum	Pittosporum tobira	
Poison ivy	Toxicodendron radicans	
Pokeweed, inkberry	Phytolacca americana	
Potato plant (leaves, sprouts, peelings)	Solanum tuberosum	
Pregnant onion	Orithogalum caudatum	
Privet	Ligustrum japonicum	
Ranunculus	Ranunculus	Minor concern for people; concern for animals
Rhododendron (many varieties; wild and cultivated)	Rhododendron	
Rhubarb (leaves)	Rheum rhaponticum	
Rosary bean or pea	Abrus precatorius	
Sago palm	Cycas revoluta	
Schefflera	Brassaia actinophylla	Minor concern for people; concern for animals
Silver mound	Artemisia schmidtiana	Moderate concern for people; concern for animals

Table 3   Some Toxic Outdoor Plants (continued)

COMMON NAME	SCIENTIFIC NAME	TOXICITY NOTES
Snow-on-the-mountain	Euphorbia marinata	Moderate concern for people; concern for animals
Spruce tree	Picea species	Concern for animals
St. Johnswort	Hypericum perforatum	
Star of Bethlehem	Ornithogalum arabicum	
String of beads	Senecio	
Sweet pea	Lathyrus odoratus	Minor concern for people; concern for animals
Tobacco, tree tobacco, flowering tobacco, cultivated tobacco	Nicotiana glauca, N. tabacum	
Tomato (leaves, stems, flowers)	Lycopersicon esculentum	
Tuberose	Polianthes tuberose	Minor concern for people; concern for animals
Vinca	Vinca major, V. minor	
Walnut tree, leaves, bark, roots	Juglans nigra	
Windflower	Anemone japonica	Minor concern for people; concern for animals
Wintersweet	Acokanthera species	
Wisteria	Wisteria floribunda	
Yew, Pacific, Florida, Canada, Japanese and other varieties	Taxus varieties	

turn? Is the soil free of large stones and dead stalks?

- What was planted in the raised bed last year? Are there plants that might be coming up again this year (e.g., perennials, biennials)?
- If you need more raised beds, where could they be located?

Choosing Raised Bed Location, Styles, and Soil

The shape, height, width and length of a raised bed are important, as well as where it is placed. Construction lumber and methods are vital issues. Discuss the construction with the Maintenance Department, and any other members of the Plant Committee and the Neighborhood team members. The right type of soil is another vital factor to consider for successful planting seasons and resident satisfaction. As in all learning situations, do your research before deciding. Take into account the following items:

Location

- Are the raised beds against a wall, in a corner, or freestanding?

Style and Design Considerations

- **Height** should comfortably accommodate a person sitting in a wheelchair or a straight chair. Test this personally.
- A **standing-room-only bed** on a platform may be built higher than the sitting version to accommodate ambulatory residents who cannot stoop over. This type is built as a box on legs. The soil-holding box should be at least six inches deep. Since soil in the box will dry out faster, water should be easily obtained and shallow-rooted crops considered.
- For either type of raised bed, the bed should be reachable from at least one side. In this case, the residents should be able to reach comfortably across the width, from front to back, and be able to move from one end of

the bed to the other without obstruction. If the bed can only be reached from three sides, the residents must be able to reach to the plants in back.

- Ideally, the bed can be tended from any side, with the ability to reach from the side to the middle, and to place several wheelchairs or straight chairs around the perimeter, parallel to the sides of the bed.

- Provide sufficient space between beds for wheelchair accessibility.

- All edges should be smooth with no splinters, sharp corners, or rough edges.

- Examine the ground surface. Is it smooth and level? away from uneven edges?

- Consider the material used to build the bed. The terms *nontoxic* and *treated wood* mean different things to different commercial outlets—even to different organic gardening experts. Synthetic wood is nontoxic and practically maintenance-free. See *Build or purchase raised beds* for more information.

- Cinder blocks as building material produce wide sides. They have holes where seeds can be planted, but they also reduce usable gardening space.

- The width of the sides of the bed will add or subtract from the actual growing space. The wider the wall, the greater the need for residents to reach farther to tend to plants. Remember arthritic joints have a limited ability to extend.

- Provide for good drainage with holes drilled at intervals in the bottom of the bed.

Soil

The easiest soil to use is a commercially prepared, lightweight soil mixture. It reduces soil compaction, promotes easier cultivation by the residents, has fewer weeds, and offers a good pathway for root systems. *Do not use topsoil by itself.* For deep raised beds, a good bagged topsoil may be used to fill the bottom third of the bed, then add a lightweight mixture leaving a few inches below the rim. One or two inches of sifted compost added to the surface of the bed will add the natural bacteria and nutrients that plants need.

Build or Purchase Raised Beds

1. Review the Plant Committee's organic gardening method policy.

2. Consider the possible consequences of using chemically treated wood for beds containing edible crops.

3. According to *Organic Gardening Magazine*[1] (1999) treated wood (CCA-treated; also known as *pressure treated*) contains "potentially hazardous amounts of arsenic." This "potent carcinogen" can deposit harmful amounts of arsenic on the hands and skin of people as they work with it in construction projects. As a finished structure, the arsenic continues to rub off on the hands and skin of people touching it. Hazardous amounts may also leach into soil surrounding the wood.

4. Investigate various types of untreated, rot-resistant woods such as cedar and locust, wood treated without the use of arsenic, and synthetic lumber made of recycled plastic and wood fiber.

5. Consider livestock water troughs as alternatives to raised beds. These are constructed of galvanized steel or molded plastic.

Tools and Equipment for Outdoor Gardens and Resident TLC

Every gardener has a favorite tool story. Gather this information from residents, team members, and volunteers. Then collect all the actual garden tools available for the individual Neighborhood, and compare with the following list. If all Neighborhoods will be sharing the same set of tools at different times, then ground rules will need to be laid by a representative from each Neighborhood.

---

[1] *Organic Gardening Magazine* has compiled a list of scientific articles relating to the dangers of using pressure treated lumber. Send $2 to OG Treated Wood Woes, 33 E. Minor St., Emmaus, PA 18098.

Tools are precious things and must be cared for and kept secure.

- ❏ Tiller (may be borrowed or rented)
- ❏ Steel-tined rake
- ❏ Sharp-pointed, long-handled shovel
- ❏ Trowels (several; should be comfortable, lightweight, sturdy)
- ❏ Child-sized tools
- ❏ Garden gloves (several pairs)
- ❏ Hoes or other cultivating tools such as a Dutch hoe (long-handled for ground beds; short-handled for raised beds)
- ❏ Lightweight, long-handled, dial-selection watering wand. Quality pays off here.
- ❏ Hose (flexible and appropriate length)
- ❏ Pruners
- ❏ An individual outdoor water faucet key which can be removed when not in use and secured where accessible to staff gardeners
- ❏ Reference books

These basics will be sufficient to start. The need for additional equipment and tools would be a good project to present to local garden or civic clubs. Be certain of the reason and use for the item requested before asking for it. The list might include:

- ❏ Seed-starting supplies
- ❏ Resident friendly, specialized tools
- ❏ Child-sized wheelbarrows
- ❏ Galvanized plant markers and a label maker for creating plant labels
- ❏ Automatic watering system
- ❏ Children's and specialty gardening books
- ❏ Tomato cages
- ❏ Trellises and arbors
- ❏ Stepping stones
- ❏ Vinyl garden bed edging
- ❏ No-maintenance fencing
- ❏ Small gas-powered cultivator (if previous ones were rented or borrowed)
- ❏ Seed planter
- ❏ Compost bins
- ❏ Hand-held spreader for wildflower seeding and lime spreading
- ❏ Duster/sprayer for organic fungicides and insect spray
- ❏ A cold frame

Planning for New Plants: A Window View for All Seasons

Watching the world from a window seat is a form of entertainment for many residents. As the garden beds are planned, consider their location in relation to the residents' window seating areas. Smaller beds might be located on various sides of the facility in order to provide residents with growing and changing scenery. The practicality of scattered locations will need to be considered.

Rather than scattered garden beds, the focus of window viewing could be interesting shrubs, blooming trees, and birdhouses. Research bloom times, autumn leaf colors, and winter shapes and textures of dried materials such as grasses. The bare-branch forms of twisted shrubs and small trees provide interest and variety during the cold months, and picturesque shapes when covered in a blanket of snow. Old favorites such as lilacs, spice bushes, pussy willows, and forsythia can contribute to reminiscence and fragrant breezes entering open windows in the spring.

Choosing New Garden Sites

When choosing the location for a new flower and/or vegetable garden including ground beds, raised beds, and containers, keep these things in mind:

- The size of the bed, the time involved, and staff and volunteers needed to maintain it
- Exposure to at least six hours of sun—more is better
- Accessible to residents
- Away from shadows and large roots of trees and shrubs (if possible)
- Away from the most distant roots of a walnut tree. Walnut tree roots secrete an acid that

inhibits the growth of many plants including vegetables, flowers, azaleas, and rhododendrons (Creasy, 1982).

- Well-drained soil
- Close to a water source
- Easily viewed (at least in part) from inside the Home
- Able to be protected from domestic and/or wildlife intruders

Annuals, Perennials, Bulbs, and Shrubs

For year-round interest, the outdoor gardens need plants, flowers, herbs, fruit, and vegetables that grow, bloom, and produce at different times from early spring through late fall. In warmer climates, residents and staff are blessed with year-round growing. Window views will give residents changing textures and colors from month to month, week to week, and, early in the season, from day to day.

When making the selection for plants, flowers, fruits, herbs and vegetables, keep these things in mind:

Annuals (flowers, herbs, vegetables, and fruits) last for one season. Their roots don't survive winter. Annuals provide excellent and long-lasting color. *Pinching back* the growing tip when first planted will produce a fuller plant. Deadheading old blooms before they go to seed will produce a steady supply of blooms. Hardy annuals bloom early and late in cooler temperatures.

Perennials either die back over the winter while their roots survive, or retain their foliage during colder months. They grow larger each year and eventually need dividing. Many perennials bloom while others have only foliage; perennial vegetables or fruits have both. Perennial flowers have a limited blooming season that can be lengthened by deadheading the faded blooms. Perennial herbs have varying sizes of blooms, which when removed, will keep the foliage production strong.

Bulbs are considered hardy or nonhardy. Hardy means they can stay in the ground all year and produce flowers during the appropriate season. Nonhardy bulbs need to be planted in the spring and taken up in the fall to avoid freezing.

Shrubs are usually hardy, and can have fragrant, colorful flowers, interesting leaves, and even attractive bare branches in the winter. Some shrubs drop their leaves in the fall, while others are evergreen. Shrubs may bloom only once during the year, or may have continuous blooms that are heavier at times, and do not need to have their blooms deadheaded.

Consider having some of each of the above. A simple drawing of the garden bed with approximate bloom times and producing dates indicated will give the gardeners an idea of how the garden will change during the seasons. The plan should provide for constant color and crop variety. Vegetables, flowers, herbs, and fruit can be grown in the same garden bed. Ask a Master Gardener or horticulturist to assist with the planning phase.

Keep the eventual size of your trees, shrubs, and crops in mind. Don't plant too close to the building. Some varieties stay compact; others vine and take over a large area. Perennials grow larger each year, and eventually need dividing.

Crops and Considerations for Deep Raised Beds for People in Wheelchairs

- Soil in raised beds warms up faster which allows for earlier planting.
- Design the boxes with excellent drainage.
- Replenish soil as needed. Finished compost will add natural organisms and nutrients to the soil.
- Plan the layout of the garden for maximum light exposure.
- Trellises and cascading crops will increase growing volume.
- Consider annuals over perennials for crop rotation and use of space.
- Use colorful, contrasting, spicy salad greens. There are many new varieties available.
- Cool weather crops (e.g., lettuce, broccoli, dwarf peas, onions, radishes) allow for earlier planting.
- For vining crops, look for compact, productive types with fewer leaves.

- Plant edible annual flowers such as nasturtiums, pansies, marigolds ('Lemon Gem' and 'Tangerine Gem'), dwarf calendula, tuberous begonias, and dwarf lavender (Creasy, 1999).
- Compact annual and perennial herbs (e.g., basil, chives, dwarf dill, lemon thyme, parsley) can be used in sensory stimulation and food activities.
- Mini-vegetables for space saving can increase the vegetable selection.

Crops and Considerations for Standing-Room Raised Beds

- Early, slow bolting spring greens such as specialty/mesclun greens which offer a variety of taste and color.
- Small radishes, mini-carrots, and other similar short-root veggies.
- Miniature head lettuce, radicchio, bush-type or patio cherry tomatoes.
- Try a container garden collection packet (found in catalogs).
- Medium height flowers for picking and arranging (e.g., zinnias, blue salvia, dwarf dahlias, verbena, pinks, pentas).
- Compact herbs (e.g., parsley, basil, chives, summer savory, dwarf dill, small starts of scented geraniums). See *Knowing and growing those fantastic herbs* (p. 84).
- Be sure that a water source is nearby and that the watering wand is easy to hold.
- How and where will the water drain?

What Do the Residents Want to Grow?

Encourage residents to suggest favorite crops and flowers. Some of them may even have specific varieties and catalogs to offer. Go through general categories of vegetables and common flowers with the residents, and ask for ideas.

Relating various vegetables to prepared foods may trigger some response, such as corn beef and cabbage, wilted lettuce salad, snap beans cooked with bacon, or split pea soup with ham.

Ask about the kinds of flowers the residents grew as children, and what flowers their mothers grew. What were some of the old-fashioned names of flowers? Did they enter 4H flower and produce competitions? Did they grow the flowers in the vegetable garden or by themselves?

What about memories of herb gardens? Were herbs used as home remedies?

Do Staff Members Have Any Special Requests for Crops or Flowers?

Vegetable and flower suggestions can be requested at the Neighborhood meetings or through posters circulated asking for the staff's ideas for crops. Maybe John from Maintenance really likes hot peppers and has a favorite type, or the evening nurse has a great salad recipe that uses yellow pear and cherry tomatoes. Future plans could include a harvest cookout using the garden produce.

Functional Crops

Functional crops might be an important issue. If there isn't much space for growing outside, specific choices will need to be made for the best use of that space. Consider these:

- Crops chosen by residents
- Crops for food activities
- Edible flowers for fun dishes; flowers to cut for table arrangements
- Herbs and flowers for drying to use in arrangements and wreaths
- Plants to attract wildlife
- Plants grown from seed to sell to staff and visitors
- Flowers and herbs for sensory stimulation (e.g., aroma, touch)
- Crops for children and resident interaction
- Crops for resident animals

Plants to Grow for Animals

A variety of vegetables are nutritious for pets such as rabbits and guinea pigs. Some dogs even like an occasional carrot. Pet caregivers must be certain that these vegetables are appropriate for each animal and are offered in the right amounts. The wrong kind of vegetable or too much of one can make a rabbit very ill. Check with the Home's veterinarian before feeding any fresh vegetable to an animal.

Getting Freebies or Reduced Prices

Garden clubs and civic organizations are likely sources for items such as tools, books, garden accessories, children's tools, and monetary donations. Presentations can be made to any potential giving group where the least expectation will be a routine donation in exchange for the program. Fliers can be sent to each club with a summary of the presentation and photos or drawings of the Home's gardening activities.

The emphasis of interaction with children is always very appealing to potential donors. Start taking slides and photos early in the gardening year, and include many scenes of children and elders together.

Local garden centers usually have unsold seed packets or loose seed. Ask early in the season if these could be donated or offered at reduced cost to the facility. Inquire about additional donations or "deals." In the fall, when unsold perennials are being cut back and divided to winter in the garden center's greenhouse, the greenhouse manager might agree to share the extras.

Starting Seeds Indoors

Review *Artificial lighting for year-round growing* (pp. 43–45) for suggestions about how to set up light shelves. Seeds started in late winter or early spring will need twelve to sixteen hours of light each day.

When the residents have contributed their requests for crops or indoor plants to be grown from seed and the staff has suggested a few choices, the seeds can be purchased or collected from other growers.

When choosing what seeds to grow for the first time (or to grow again as a result of a successful crop from last season), consider the following:

Space/Area Issues

- Where will the crops be grown? inside? outside? in a raised or ground-level bed? in containers?
- How large an area is needed for each crop?
- How much space is available on the growing shelves?
- Where to locate the seedlings once they outgrow the light shelves: a southern window exposure? a cold frame? a protected area outside?
- How many flats of each crop should be grown?
- Which seeds are to be started *inside* and when? Which seeds can be sown directly into *outside* beds and when?

Some flower and vegetable seeds need a head start indoors under lights in order to produce blooms and fruit within the growing zone's frost-free months. For example, begonias and impatiens need several weeks of growth indoors before being planted outside after the last frost in order to enjoy blooms early in the season. On the other hand, annual flowers such as zinnias can be planted directly into warm outdoor soil after the danger of frost has passed, and they will grow rapidly and produce blooms for the majority of the season. Some annual seeds such as calendula and peas sprout in cool soil and are frost resistant. This gives the gardener the advantage of an early start and less work. Check the seed packets for instructions about appropriate planting times for your area.

What People Want/Plant Considerations

- The use of each crop
- Variety of crops grown
- Appropriate times to start seeds

Some vegetable and flower seeds need to be sown indoors in late winter or early spring. Warm weather crop seeds can be started outside after soil has warmed. Houseplant seeds can be started at almost any time of year.

Staff Resources, Equipment, and Supplies to Consider

- Increased time for staff/residents to water, tend to, and transplant seedlings

- Sources of seeds (e.g., catalogs, garden centers, plant societies, local gardeners)

- Purchase of timer for grow lights

- Purchase of **sterile** seed-starting soil which contains **fertilizer**

- Purchasing seeds, growing containers, and time-release fertilizer or a soil mix that contains fertilizer

- Organic methods for fertilizing can be used, but may be more expensive and time-consuming. Look into using fish emulsion or seaweed extract. The use of organic fertilizer such as compost, bone meal, and green sand in *outside* garden beds is a more critical issue due to the presence of living organisms and worms in the soil which need organic methods to thrive

- Using on-hand containers such as milk and juice cartons for young transplants

- Donation of other materials

Basic Seed Starting Reminders

- Have all supplies and seeds ready.

- Make a list of seeds in the garden logbook. Include information about when they are planted and where (indoors and outside). Insert a plastic label into each flat with the plant's name and date the seeds were sown.

- If this is a new experience, start with easy to handle seeds. Be realistic about the number of varieties of seeds and the number of flats.

- Will seeds be planted (sprinkled) onto a **flat** of soil without separate compartments, and then picked out and transplanted when the seedlings are large enough? Or will the seeds will be planted in divided cell packs or small containers? The number of seeds per container will depend on the size of the seed. Consider how many seeds of each crop to plant and that transplanting takes time.

- All containers must have drainage holes.

- Keep all seed packets for planting, spacing, care, mature height and width information.

- Have a good seed starting book available with specific directions for each variety of seed. Some seeds need cold treatment, soaking, or nicking of the seed coat before planting. Not all packets explain this. See *Park's Success with Seeds* (Reilly, 1992), and *Resources* (p. 132, 135).

- Plant seeds in **moist** soil at the recommended depth found on their packet. Cover with a clear plastic lid or tent, and place in a warm location. A southern window exposure or the heat of fluorescent grow lights approximately eight inches above the planted seeds should be enough. If you need to use lights, leave them on during the coolest part of a 24-hour period, and turn them off when the air temperature rises above sixty-five degrees. Pay attention to directions about seeds that need to be covered or uncovered when planted. If the seeds need light to germinate, leave the lights on continuously until the seeds sprout, then keep the lights on for 12–14 hours a day from early morning to evening as the seedlings grow.

- A temperature drop of a few degrees at night should not be a problem. If the soil cools too much, though, seeds may not sprout. Normal Home temperatures should be sufficient. A maximum–minimum thermometer can record the lowest and highest temperatures within 24 hours. This instrument can track your seed-starting environment temperatures and create an interesting activity for the residents as they monitor the readings. Garden centers or horticultural supply catalogs usually carry these (see *Resources,* p. 132).

- Once the seeds have sprouted, set the fluorescent light timer to be on at least 12 hours a day. The seedlings need to be 8–10 inches from the light tube. If the seedlings look spindly, move the flat closer to the light, or increase the amount of time the lights are on.

- Air circulation is very important to prevent a disease called *damping off* (an orange-colored mold-like growth on the soil surface which can kill seedlings very quickly). A small fan will keep air moving to help reduce the chance of this.

- When seedlings have their first or second "true" leaves, transplant them to individual cell packs or containers, two to three per cell. (Mini milk containers also work well.) Depending on the expected size of the plant, the seedlings can later be thinned to one plant per cell by trimming away the smaller seedlings with scissors—don't pull them out. In the case of small mature plants such as sweet alyssum, they can be left to grow together.

- Move growing plants to a cold frame or a protected outdoor spot to "harden off" before placing the new plants into garden beds. Plants need to adjust to the outside temperature, sun, and wind before being planted. This adjustment time will produce sturdier plants. Gradually increase exposure to sun and wind, and reduce the frequency of watering to allow the plants to adjust to life on their own.

- Review the spacing suggestions on the seed packet before planting in garden beds. Tiny seedlings grow into large plants.

Using a Cold Frame

A cold frame is simply a bottomless box with slanted sides and a hinged plastic or glass top, rather like a mini-greenhouse. Cold frames allow the grower to place seedlings outdoors to help them gradually adjust to varying weather conditions. An **automatic cold frame lid opener** is highly recommended to reduce the need to manually raise and lower the lid to prevent overheating during the day or chilling at night. Without the automatic opener, a staff member will need to be constantly on the alert to raise and lower the lid according to the outside temperatures.

Discuss building a cold frame with the Maintenance Department and other creative members of the Plant Committee. It is not a difficult project

and can be built for under $100. Kits can be purchased for a bit more. Be aware that automatic lid openers can lift only a limited number of pounds.

Using Low Maintenance, Easy-Care Gardening Methods

Balancing the care and upkeep of plants and outdoor gardens with the priorities of residents and their needs is a challenging task for staff involved in a gardening environment. As the gardening routine becomes established and the gardeners become comfortable with what to do, when, and how to do it, the true rewards of working together in nature will be enjoyed. Eventually, the staff, residents, and volunteers will want to take on more complicated gardening projects. Meanwhile, start with easy, familiar crops, small spaces, comfortable tools, and work-reducing approaches.

Plan these things on paper and through discussions with the Plant Committee members, residents, and other staff:

❏ A seasonal plan for flowers, vegetables, ornamentals, and their use.

❏ The outdoor gardeners' maintenance schedule with backups for vacation and illness.

❏ A weekly calendar of gardening tasks and resident interactions.

❏ The involvement of knowledgeable volunteers and helpers.

❏ Inform all residents, staff, and families about the garden's progress, and how they can help.

❏ Hold mini training sessions for the people participating in gardening activities.

❏ Use tools suggested by an occupational therapist. Research adaptive measures for residents with physical and visual challenges.

❏ Research and discuss various types of raised beds and containers. Involve residents in testing and choosing these items.

❏ Order catalogs that feature adaptive tools.

Out in the Garden, Try These Things:

❏ Prepare the soil well. Lay stepping stones or boards to avoid compacting soil.

❏ Mulch well to reduce the need to water, keep soil loose, and reduce weeding time.

❏ Water early in the morning when possible. Spray the under side of leaves to discourage mites while watering.

❏ Spot-check plants routinely for insects or diseases.

❏ Use organic pest controls at first sign of problems.

❏ Feed plants routinely. Use finished compost as a side dressing, purchase bagged aged manure, or other organic fertilizers.

❏ Keep the garden free from debris such as dead leaves, blossoms and rotting fruit.

❏ Start a compost pile.

❏ Cultivate gently around the base of plants.

❏ Pick off old blossoms.

Working with Tools:

❏ Wrap tool handles with foam tubes. Paint handles yellow or wrap with yellow tape and paint or mark black dots or stripes on the yellow areas.

❏ For residents with limited dexterity and bending ability, use seeding devices such as wheeled seed sowers (found in catalogs), large-holed salt shakers filled with seeds mixed with sand, or long PVC tubes for guiding peas and beans into a row trench (see Figure 5).

❏ Select a lightweight, soft spray, long-handled watering wand to attach to the garden hose. The "dial-a-spray" styles are usually too forceful for gentle watering by residents.

❏ Use ropes and pulleys for hanging baskets.

❏ Try a gel additive to increase water content in smaller containers and pots, and reduce the frequency of watering.

❏ Keep soft ties available for tying plants that need support. Old socks and panty hose cut to the desired size work well for this.

❏ Carry tools in a bucket or caddie. Store tools safely.

Place hollow pipe in seed furrow   Drop seed through pipe.

Figure 5   Hollow Pipe Seeding

❏ Use a wheelchair tool caddie. Fasten a plastic tool caddy to the vertical front portion of the armrests with Velcro straps. The caddy can rest in the resident's lap with little concern about its slipping off. See Figure 6 (p. 76).

❏ Investigate hose storage devices.

❏ Use sturdy cages, stakes, and trellises for tall plants, vines, and crops.

❏ Learn and use good body mechanics when digging, weeding, shoveling, hoeing, carrying, and performing other duties in the garden.

❏ Schedule an occupational therapist to demonstrate tool use and body mechanics for residents, staff, and volunteers

Planning Intergenerational Activities

Outdoor gardening activities are featured in the Gardening Calendars with selected explanations. A few things to keep in mind:

Preparation

• Review the activity plan with the residents before the children arrive.

• Ask for assistance from able and willing residents to make preparations such as filling washed milk cartons with soil.

Figure 6   Wheelchair Tool Caddie

- Have soil premoistened if seeds are to be planted in containers.

Safety Considerations

- Review safety issues such as toxic plants in the garden and the probability of young toddlers putting garden materials (such as pretty flowers, stones, soil, and sticks) in their mouths, the possibility of stinging insects, the dangers of nearby traffic, and any hazards from uneven or damaged sidewalks.

- Use only nontoxic, untreated seeds.

- Use only a water spray for controlling insects at the time of the children's visit. Use recommended organic insect spray at a later time when the children are not present.

- Provide a comfortable, shady place outdoors for the elders and children to work on garden projects such as potting up, making bouquets or having a show-and-tell session.

- Obtain recommendations from the child daycare staff about the children's seating comfort and temperature tolerance.

- Keep seats, paths and patios cleared of tools, hoses and other equipment.

- Have a plan for washing dirty hands.

- Expect the children to help clean up and put away tools and supplies.

- Formulate a first-aid policy and procedure with the child day center staff. Know where to find first-aid supplies.

- Have drinking water available. Serve it routinely on warm days.

Staff and Resources

- Schedule extra volunteers when taking a group of children outside. One volunteer to four to six children is a fair rule-of-thumb depending on the age and behavior of the children.

- Share the cost of materials with the daycare center, or rotate the provision of the paper, seeds, containers, child-sized garden tools, and other items used during garden activities.

- Don't forget to call the newspaper to feature special gardening events with children and residents.

Wildlife in the Garden

Every residential home has some form of wildlife in its garden. As the outdoor gardens become a more personal part of the Home's living environment, residents and staff will notice the native birds and animals, and will want to attract and observe their favorites. The wildlife in residential gardens around the country is as different as individual homes and their locations. Cardinals, blue jays, and sparrows will be a common sight in the east and midwest, while bird feeders in the western mountain states will attract northern mockingbirds, California towhees, and black-headed grosbeaks. Squirrels will take shelter in large trees, and chipmunks and garden snakes may enjoy the protection and warmth of a rock pile. If the Home is fortunate enough to have a small pond, its frog and turtle dwellers will bring back childhood memories of rural life.

When people elect to feed wildlife they take on a satisfying experience as well as an admirable responsibility. The Plant Committee can include the ways and means of attracting wildlife in the overall planning of the outdoor gardens. An employee of the state's Division of Wildlife or a local naturalist could be invited to discuss the basics of backyard wildlife management. Some important issues for the Committee to consider and investigate:

- Preferences of the residents—benefits of variety and spontaneity from wildlife.

- Planning the garden layout and location of resident seating areas, raised flower and vegetable beds, birdfeeding stations, rock and brush piles, and future areas to develop.

- Purchase or construction of bird and squirrel feeders (budget or donation).

- Time needed to care for feeders, and means of supplying feed (budget or donation).

- The surrounding neighbors' reactions to increased wildlife population.

- Natural food plants, shrubs, and trees in the garden for animals such as birds, butterflies, rabbits, squirrels, and water animals.

- The risks of luring wild animals to the garden such as residents' and children's safety issues, bird droppings, rabies, possible damage to crops, lawns and buildings.

- Prevention and management of unwanted wild visitors.

- Seasonal issues such as continuous feeding in winter; joy of watching baby birds and animals, and continual need to supply water.

- Enjoyment and public relations value of becoming a "certified backyard wildlife habitat."

- Support of and excellent information supplied by each state's Department of Natural Resources, Division of Wildlife, and other private conservation associations.

Part 3: Digging In

Preparing the Soil

No garden soil is perfect, but with some basic TLC (tender, loving cultivation), any kind of soil can be improved. Before serious gardening is attempted, the Outdoor Garden Team would benefit from information gained by a **soil test**. This test is done by the County Extension Office, and will require a reasonable fee. The Extension personnel will provide instructions for taking garden soil samples. Ideally, the sample should be taken in the fall, so that any correcting can be done before spring planting.

The results will show whether the soil is sweet (alkaline) or sour (acid), and will list the nitrogen, phosphorous and potassium content. This may sound like a lot of trouble, but the Team will be avoiding trouble by knowing the condition of the soil from the start. When the test results are obtained, ask the Master Gardener on the Plant Committee or call the Master Gardener station at the Extension Office to find out what ingredients are needed to improve the soil. By explaining to the Master Gardener volunteer what crops are to be grown in the individual beds, the appropriate amendments can be made to the soil. If the Committee has decided to grow organically with no added chemicals, this choice must be made clear to the person recommending soil improvement methods.

If the flower or vegetable bed is to be **turned for the first time**, be sure to enlist strong backs and sharp shovels. Depending on the condition of the soil and the size of the plot, a heavy-duty rotary tiller and a knowledgeable operator may be more appropriate. Clear out weeds, rocks, and other debris before digging or tilling. Small flower or vegetable beds can be spaded by hand to a depth of 8–10 inches. If grass is present, it can be turned under and left to rot (best done in fall), removed by machine, or hand pulled.

The addition of **organic material** is very important for the success of any garden. If the garden can be dug in the fall, spread leaves, and nontreated grass clippings (i.e., those that have *not*

been chemically fertilized or sprayed with pesticides) over the top of the bed to a depth of two to three inches, then it will be ready for spring tilling. When using grass clippings, mix them with other organic ingredients such as leaves and compost to prevent clumping. When left in a pile, grass clippings heat up quickly, smell awful, and dry into hard, leathery clumps.

The amendment of soil with manure and any materials containing manure such as soiled straw bedding must be researched and discussed by the Plant Committee and the outdoor Garden Team. Disease-causing microorganisms including *E. coli*, salmonella and tuberculosis can be transferred from animal manure, especially in its raw state, to humans. In view of this concern, the application of horse, cow, rabbit or chicken manure must be given special consideration. Only **well-rotted (composted) manure** should be used at any time. The **American Organic Standards** for compost production to kill human pathogens state that compost must reach a temperature of at least 130°F for a period of several days, be thoroughly mixed, and achieve that temperature again before finishing for a period of approximately six weeks. Any manure applied after planting should be composted manure. Only processed, pathogen-free manure should be used within thirty days of harvesting a crop. Do **not** use cat, dog, pig manure or any product associated with these animals such as used kitty litter or soiled straw bedding in gardens or compost piles. Harmful parasites may be contained in these forms of manure (Hillers, 1998, Jones, 2000).

Residents and other gardeners who are susceptible to foodborne illnesses including young children, pregnant women, and those with chronic diseases such as cancer, kidney disease and diabetes should avoid eating *uncooked* vegetables from manured gardens. Always thoroughly wash vegetables from the garden before eating raw or cooking (Hillers, 1998, Jones, 2000).

The soil report from the Cooperative Extension office may indicate the need for certain additions to the soil, and chemical fertilizers may be the standard recommendation. The Plant Team should explain their preference for **organic fertilizers and amendments** to the Extension Office. Ask the Extension Agent or a knowledgeable Master Gardener how to add things like cottonseed meal, blood meal, bone meal, and green sand. These slow-release, natural fertilizers are nontoxic to worms and good bacteria found in the soil. Find out how much of these ingredients to add and when, and the best place to buy them.

If the Plant Committee or Garden Team chooses to use the chemical fertilizer recommendations, they should remember to also add compost or good topsoil to the soil in order to provide the natural organisms needed to break down organic matter and increase soil fertility.

Plan to **mulch** the **flower garden** with whatever material is available. For a bed containing mostly flowers, hardwood mulch is appropriate. Hardwood breaks down slowly, but it removes nitrogen from the soil. To protect your plants from malnutrition, be sure to fertilize the flowers on a regular basis. **Grass clippings,** spread evenly and no more than an inch thick, will keep the soil loose and soft and provide some nutrients. If mulch is not practical, **peat moss** (*not* Michigan peat *soil*), **worked into** the top three to four inches will also keep the soil loose. Peat moss is slightly acidic, so it may affect plants that need a sweeter soil.

Mulch for the **vegetable garden** can be straw (contact local farmers), three to five layers of

> **mulch:** material used to cover soil for the purpose of retaining moisture, reducing weed growth, and keeping plant roots cool. Examples include shredded bark, grass clippings, straw, compost, cocoa hulls, black-and-white nonglossy newspaper, landscape cloth, and black plastic. The best mulches allow air and water to penetrate down to the plant's roots, and will break down into particles that plants use as food.
>
> ————————————————
>
> **to mulch:** the act of spreading mulching materials over a garden bed that contains growing plants, or that has been cleared of plants to prepare for next season's planting.

black-and-white, nonglossy newspaper, well-rotted sawdust (fresh sawdust removes nitrogen from the soil), or, if you live near a chocolate factory, cocoa bean hulls. Black plastic can be used to heat up soil prior to planting in the spring, and then removed. Plastic is not recommended for longer than a temporary cover since water and air cannot penetrate it and it does not break down.

Consider starting a **compost pile**. A member of the dietary staff will be helpful to the Plant Committee since he or she can determine the possibility of contributing kitchen vegetable scraps to the pile (no meat or meat products). Think of all those banana skins! Most city departments save leaves for composting. The Maintenance department could pick up a truckload for a starter pile. Grass clippings, which were not chemically sprayed while growing, make a good addition to compost piles as long as they are mixed in well with the other compost ingredients.

The compost pile should be no smaller than 3 feet by 3 feet to encourage the interior to heat up, decompose, and kill weed seeds and harmful bacteria. Turning the pile will speed up the process by mixing air into the pile. Ideally, turning should be done whenever new materials are added, and weekly. A long-handled garden rake with tines, a clawed cultivating tool, or a hay rake is adequate to turn a small to moderate sized pile. Sturdy sticks

compost: organic material placed in a pile and is in the process of rotting (breaking down), or has broken down to the point of being "finished." Finished compost looks like soil and has no odor.

Materials suitable for compost piles include: pulled weeds without seed heads, grass clippings that were *not* treated with chemical sprays, kitchen scraps (no meat or fat), used coffee grounds, discarded potted plants, debris from garden clean up, fallen leaves, small twigs, pet and human hair clippings, and sawdust.

to compost: to add organic material to a compost pile to allow it to break down into particles small enough for plants to use as food.

placed in a loose platform arrangement to form a base for the pile will assist to admit air. Perforated PVC piping inserted into the deepest part of the pile (2–3 pieces, depending on the size of the pile) and extending a foot or so above the top of the pile will help admit air. Stabbing the pile with a pitchfork or digging bar will also create spaces for air to enter.

If it isn't possible to turn the pile frequently, try to shovel out finished compost from the bottom of the pile and sprinkle this over the new materials as they are added to the top. This dark, crumbly soil contains microbes and fungi which help break down and digest the new additions.

Compost bins may be made from cinder blocks, rot-resistant, untreated wood, sturdy wire fencing, or the ingredients simply may be piled in an available corner of the garden. The compost will break down more rapidly if it is **turned** every one to two weeks, and a means of aeration is provided.

Preparing Raised Beds

An advantage of raised beds is the ability to have more control over the soil quality. The soil in raised beds bordered by wood or cinder blocks, or beds in large pots, bathtubs, or water troughs are easier to improve due to the limited volume of soil. All of the same practices used for improving soil in larger ground beds can be applied to the raised beds.

The objectives of improved soil are good drainage, nutrition for earthworms and crops, and ease of cultivation for residents. Even if commercial bagged **potting soil** (the type mixed with perlite, vermiculite, bark, sand, and other ingredients) is used in the raised bed, this soil will be improved by adding compost which provides natural soil bacteria and fungi. For larger raised beds bordered by wood or other material, bagged **topsoil** can be mixed with compost or other shredded materials such as leaves and grass clippings to enrich the soil already in place.

In August 2000, an Environmental Protection Agency fact sheet entitled *Asbestos-Contaminated Vermiculite* addressed the concern about the use of gardening products containing vermiculite. In the final analysis, "the likelihood of the asbestos becoming airborne, during routine use of these products, indicated that this potential exposure poses a minimal health risk to consumers." The following recommendations are given to further reduce the "low risk associated with the occasional use of vermiculite products during gardening activities:"

- Use vermiculite outdoors in a well-ventilated area.
- Keep vermiculite damp during use to reduce the amount of dust created.
- Avoid bringing dust from vermiculite into the Home on clothing.
- Use premixed potting soil, which usually contains more moisture and less vermiculite than a pure vermiculite product. This is less likely to generate dust.
- Use other soil additives such as peat, sawdust, perlite or bark.

Contact the EPA's Toxic Substances Control Act Assistance Information Service (202–554–1404) to obtain a copy of the vermiculite survey report.

Basic Vegetable Garden Plans

As the staff and residents decide what they want in the garden, they will benefit from a simple sketch of the garden layout. Include where the various vegetables, herbs, and flowers will be planted. First, draw the garden the way you think it will be in pencil. Then, after planting, make corrections on the pencil-and-paper plan. Try to use simple sketches of the actual veggies or flowers with their names under the drawings in black felt-tip pen. When planting is complete, date the drawing, and make copies to hang in the Neighborhood, and for the children to color.

When **planning the garden layout**, think about the following:

• Is there a view of the garden from inside the home?

• Will children be working with the adults?

• How will the rows be marked (e.g., laminated pictures on sticks, indelible ink signs, paint-stirring sticks, galvanized labels)?

• *Direction of the sun:* Observe where shadows fall in the morning, at noon, and during the afternoon. Prevent larger plants from casting shade by placing taller plants like tomatoes, sunflowers, pole beans, and corn in the north side of the plot.

• Think ahead to cool-season crops (e.g., lettuces, greens, radishes) being replaced by warm-weather crops. In late summer, cool-

Table 4   Companion Planting

NAME	COMPANION PLANTS	PLANTS TO AVOID WITH FIRST COLUMN
Asparagus	Parsley, basil, tomatoes	Rue
Basil	Tomatoes	
Beans, bush and pole	Carrots, beets (with bush beans), cauliflower, cucumbers, cabbages, corn (pole beans climb the stalks), marigolds, potatoes, strawberries, summer savory	Onions, garlic, chives, shallots, gladiolus, fennel
Beets	Bush beans, onions, kohlrabi	Pole beans
Broccoli	See "cabbage family"	See "cabbage family"
Cabbage family	Aromatic plants such as dill, camomile, sage, rosemary as well as potatoes, beets, and onions	Tomatoes, pole beans, strawberries
Carrots	Herbs, leeks, lettuce, onions, tomatoes	Dill
Cauliflower	See "cabbage family"	See "cabbage family"
Chives	Carrots, apple trees	
Coreopsis	Repels insects from adjacent garden plants	
Cucumber	Beans, peas, radishes, sunflowers	Aromatic herbs, potatoes
Eggplant	Bush beans	
Fennel	Plant by itself away from crops	Coriander, wormwood
Garlic	Repels borers from apple trees, insects from roses and tomatoes	Don't plant near beans and peas
Geraniums	Roses, grapes, corn	
Kohlrabi	Onions, beets, fragrant herbs, cucumbers	Strawberries, tomatoes, pole beans

season crops may again be planted to mature in the fall.

- Select a permanent spot for perennial crops such as asparagus, rhubarb, horseradish, raspberries, and strawberries.

- Follow directions on seed packets for spacing plants, or ask at the garden center when the seeds are purchased.

- Practice *companion planting*. Certain plants are good for each other, while others will stunt each other's growth. Certain plants repel insect pests, while others attract beneficial insects (see Table 4).

- Make paths wide enough for a wheelchair. Paved paths are ideal, but strips of old carpeting laid over an unpaved path will control weeds and assist the wheelchair traffic.

- Use existing fences or posts for climbing crops.

- Wrap polystyrene cups, aluminum foil collars, or toilet paper roll tubes around tomato and squash plant stems just below the soil level to discourage cut worms.

- Erect tomato cages, teepees, and stakes at the time of planting.

- Consider planting potatoes in a barrel or tire.

Table 4   Companion Planting (continued)

NAME	COMPANION PLANTS	PLANTS TO AVOID WITH FIRST COLUMN
Lettuce	Onions, strawberries, cucumbers, carrots, radishes	
Marigolds (fragrant, older varieties)	Tomatoes, beans, and around the edge of the garden to discourage nematodes (a microscopic root worm)	
Melon	Corn, sunflowers	Don't rotate with squash or cucumbers; dislikes potatoes
Nasturtiums	Squash, broccoli, potatoes, radishes, cucumbers	
Onion	All members of cabbage family, beets, strawberries, tomatoes, lettuce	Peas, beans
Parsley	Carrots, roses, tomatoes, asparagus	
Peas	Carrots, radishes, cucumbers, corn, beans, potatoes, herbs	Onion, garlic, gladiolus
Pepper, sweet	Okra	
Potatoes	Beans, corn, cabbage, horseradish, marigold, eggplant	Pumpkins, tomatoes, raspberries, squash, cucumbers, sunflower
Pumpkins	Corn	Potatoes
Radish	Beets, spinach, carrots, cucumbers, squash, melons, kohlrabi, beans, leaf lettuce	Hyssop
Tomatoes	Asparagus, basil, carrots, chives, garlic, marigold, parsley, nasturtium	No member of cabbage family, fennel, corn, or potatoes

- Choose a spot for the compost pile. Locate it out of the main traffic patterns and away from windows, but close enough to the outside door to be easily reached by staff or residents who want to add daily kitchen scraps. Enclose the pile with a wire fence on three sides. The open side should have space for a wheelbarrow to pull up to collect finished compost.

- Locate tools conveniently. Can something (e.g., an aluminum mailbox) be set up in the garden to hold smaller tools?

- Create occasional alcoves on firm ground along the garden rows to hold a sturdy chair. If the raised beds are workable while sitting, place at least one chair beside each bed.

- Think about garden art. Bird baths, trellises, a scarecrow, a sundial, a garden gate, signs, and other statuary can add interest to the landscape.

Basic Flower Garden Plans

Flowers may be in a bed by themselves or grown side-by-side with the vegetables. The residents may prefer to grow the flowers in rows for cutting or have a flowerbed designed specifically for annual and perennial flowers. Whatever the choices, consider the following:

- Observe the view of flower beds from inside the Home.

- Arrange the beds so that residents have access to touching, smelling, and cutting the flowers.

- Test and prepare the soil before planting.

- Know the light exposure for the bed and sunlight requirements for the flowers.

- Consider the advantages of organic gardening methods.

- Understand the difference between *annual* and *perennial* flowers.

- Know the temperature requirements for the flowers as they mature.

- Decide on color schemes or a multicolored plan.

- Know the height and spread of the mature plant. Keep in mind that perennials will continue to expand, but can be divided periodically.

- Know when and for how long perennials bloom.

- Keep in mind the angle of the sun. Position taller plants on the north side of the plot to prevent shading the shorter ones.

- Discuss the planting of spring and summer bulbs and their care.

- Provide stepping stones or pathways to prevent walking on the soil.

- Leave space for garden art (e.g., a fountain, birdbath, arbor, stone or ironwork) and for gates, trellises, or plants in pots.

Knowing and Growing Those Fantastic Herbs

Herbs are one of the most rewarding crops to grow. Generally, herbs are low maintenance, sturdy, and multifunctional. Their uses range from sensory stimulation to food preparation and crafts. Their folklore provides for fascinating reading and reminiscing as well.

No experience is needed to raise herbs. Be sure to ask the residents about their preferences and childhood memories. Try a few herbs the first season and experiment with seeds and plants, both annuals and perennials. Herbs can be mixed into the flowerbed or grown as companion plants among the veggies. Learning and enjoyment is guaranteed.

Herbs can be started from seed, purchased as small plants, dug from a friend's plot, or donated by herb and garden club members. For **seed-starting success**, try the following:

Basil. Start indoors according to packet directions. When seedlings are two to three inches tall, transplant into a milk carton-sized pot. Set out in a protected place or a cold frame to harden off for a week. Plant after danger of frost has past. Pinch back center growth to encourage bushy plants.

Dill. Sow in early spring directly into the garden where it is to grow. Allow some plants to go to seed for a continuous supply.

Parsley. Soak the seed in water for 24 hours prior to sowing directly into the garden in early spring. Be sure to mark the spot as these seeds are slow to sprout (about 3 weeks). These plants are decorative and blend well with colorful annuals.

'Pot' marigold or Calendula. Start indoors according to packet directions. Plant outside after hardening off for a week. May be directly sown into the garden bed as well.

Some herbs to try as **purchased or donated plants**:

Rosemary. This tender perennial requires full sun. It's slow growing but has a marvelous aroma. Bring it inside when the weather gets frosty. Rosemary needs good drainage, air circulation, and the brightest window, especially when grown indoors.

Lavender. This hardy perennial requires full sun. Leave adequate space since it will fill out more each year. Its flowers make an excellent addition to sachet bags, and it is also good for potpourri due to its soothing aroma.

Chives. This hardy perennial likes sun. It sets pretty flowers in Spring and will rebloom if its flowers are cut before going to seed. Chives discourage aphids when planted under roses. A quarter-sized plug will grow into a large plant.

Sage (several types). Garden sage is a hardy, attractive, fuzzy plant with a strong aroma.

Sweet Annie. This annual self-seeds easily. It's **not edible,** but is great for dried arrangements and wreaths. Its wonderful aroma changes as it dries.

Silver Queen artemisia. This hardy perennial requires full sun and needs lots of space. Like Sweet Annie, it is **not edible,** but it is excellent for wreaths and dried arrangements. Silver Queen has been known to cause hay fever-like reactions in some people.

Mints (many types). This hardy perennial likes full sun to part shade, and some moisture. Plant several kinds and locate them where spreading will not be a problem. To control spreading, mints can be planted in a large plastic or metal bucket with several holes drilled in bottom for drainage, then sink the container into the ground to keep the roots from spreading.

Some herb **maintenance tips** to keep in mind:

- Invest in or borrow a good herb book that contains detailed growing instructions as well as uses for herbs.
- Use bug sprays only as a last resort and then **only** organic formulas. A soap spray should be sufficient.
- Most herbs require well-drained, slightly alkaline (sweet) soil. Well-tilled, common garden soil is fine.
- Do not fertilize soil around herbs. The addition of compost is beneficial once a season.
- Do not mix peat moss or pine needles into soil since this raises the acidity level.
- If mulch is used, scatter it thinly. Overly moist soil will rot the roots and produce mold.
- Keep flower spikes picked off. Don't allow herbs to go to seed except as a means of producing more plants (i.e., self-seeding), or when the seed is used in food preparation.
- Low-growing herbs such as thyme love to climb over rocks.
- Gather herbs for fresh use before noon. This is when the oils are up in the leaves and stems.
- Research when to cut herbs for drying.
- Cut back plants or pinch out growing tips periodically to produce bushier plants.

- Water only as needed. Seedlings need more frequent watering, but large and/or woody herbs appreciate some dryness.
- Contact herb clubs for garden volunteers.

Using Organic Gardening Methods

Organic gardening is the most practical way to take care of gardens in a setting where the safety and well-being of people, curious pets, and wildlife is a concern. Dr. Bill Thomas, founder of the Eden Alternative, states

> *Safety is critically important.* That's why we always encourage organic methods as a first approach. Chemicals can be applied but should be used sparingly and carefully.

It is also far more rewarding (and fun!) to see the living results of composting, companion planting, and natural bug control methods. At state survey time for nursing homes, the garden supply cabinet can be unlocked to reveal the safest possible methods of pest and disease control.

Excellent sources of information exist about specific uses of organic materials (see *References and resources,* p. 134). The following list contains some basic guidelines:

- During Plant Committee meetings, discuss the use of natural methods and/or chemicals for the indoor and outdoor gardens. Invite a knowledgeable Cooperative Extension agent, Master Gardener, and/or organic gardener to attend these meetings.
- Visit garden centers and investigate available organic gardening products.
- Order organic gardening catalogs and read their recommendations.
- Subscribe to an organic gardening magazine.
- Develop a personal viewpoint for using natural indoor and outdoor gardening methods.
- Connect with a local organic gardening club.

Also consider specific natural gardening practices, such as:

- Practice companion planting.

- Only use homemade and commercial natural insect control **after reading** instructions and precautions on the entire label.
- Make and use a compost pile.
- Plant native flowers and shrubs to attract wildlife.
- Use safe wildlife control devices such as fencing, hanging tin plates, netting, and sprinkling blood meal.
- Useg soil-improving methods.
- Apply natural fertilizers in the indoor and outdoor gardens **only after reading** the entire label.
- Hold in-services on these topics.

Setting Up a Schedule for Garden Care

Garden maintenance can be divided into different tasks for each day of the week and modified according to the weather, time of the year, and staff or volunteers available. The primary gardening tasks will be watering, weeding, and plant grooming. Since many people will be involved, no one person or group should have more than a portion of the work to accomplish. As crops mature, the spontaneous pleasure of cutting lettuce, pulling radishes, clipping broccoli, snipping squash blossoms, and picking tomatoes will fall into the daily task schedule.

Interested residents should be asked to accompany staff into the garden as often as possible. Being involved in the gardening experience on a continuing basis will provide joy and satisfaction, especially to those residents who participated from the beginning.

When setting up the schedule, the Gardeners can keep in mind the following:

- Orient staff or volunteers before assigning them to garden care. Make sure they know what was planted where, and the difference between weeds and garden plants.
- Consider sharing the garden care among all shifts.
- Post the schedule where it can be seen by everyone. Include backup names and phone

numbers for illness, vacations and unexpected gaps in help.

- Create a weekly checklist for gardening tasks, laminate it, and hang it with the schedule (e.g., tie up plants, deadhead blooms, weed, water).

- Wait until the foliage is dry before working in the garden. Disease spreads more readily in wet conditions.

- Cool weather slows down the need for water.

- Mulching will keep soil moist and discourage weeds.

- The task of watering should be assigned and not left to chance. Schedule sufficient time to water everything thoroughly.

- Gardeners will need to water containers and raised beds more than once a week. Mulching and water-absorbing gel will reduce watering needs for containers and raised beds.

- Be consistent with garden care each week. Walk through the entire garden to inspect it, even if it appears that nothing special needs to be done.

Routine Garden Care

- ❏ Laminate and attach a garden task list to the schedule clipboard.

- ❏ Routine tasks may include: weeding, deadheading blooms, tying up sprawling or vining plants, thinning out foliage, spraying or dusting for insect pests, picking off insects or caterpillars, spreading mulch, cultivating soil, cutting back plants, disposing of debris, turning compost pile, harvesting crops, and cutting flowers.

- ❏ Discuss with the residents which tasks they would like to do.

- ❏ Provide sun protection for residents and staff as needed.

- ❏ Have drinking water available.

- ❏ Provide adaptive tools for residents as needed.

- ❏ Keep the tools where they can be reached easily.

- ❏ Clean the tools and put them away in the same place after each use.

- ❏ Consider recording the date, names of the gardeners, and "routine" or "special" tasks completed on the weekly schedule.

Watering the Garden Plants

What does it mean to "water thoroughly?" Experience will teach the gardener how much water to apply, and when to apply it. Meanwhile, the following points should be considered:

- Raised beds and containers dry out faster than ground-level beds.

- Mulched beds and containers hold water longer than unmulched areas.

- Commercially prepared water-holding gels or "beads" can be added to pots and containers to conserve moisture.

- Organic matter mixed into the soil will help to retain moisture.

- A gentle stream of water applied to the base of the plant gets water to the roots faster and more efficiently than a spray applied over the top of the foliage.

- Water early in the morning to give the plants time to dry.

- Apply a firm spray to the undersides of leaves to discourage mites and white flies.

- Occasional cultivation of the soil around the plants enables water to soak in more easily.

- Wilted plants and dry soil below the surface are signs of dry roots. Soggy soil and wilted plants are signs of root rot.

- Sunny days, rainy days, full sun, shade, temperature, wind, thickness of leaves, size and age of the plant, and different people caring for the plants, all play a part in the plants' need for water.

- A high quality hose, comfortable nozzle, accessible water source, and easy hose storage contribute to enjoyable and appropriate watering of the garden.

Figure 7   Sample Outdoor Garden Schedule

DAY OF THE WEEK	SUGGESTED GARDEN TASKS
MONDAY	• Before noon, water beds, plant containers and compost pile as needed (check soil for moisture). • Once plants have dried, deadhead flowers; pick ripe vegetables.
TUESDAY	• Pull weeds; discard weeds in compost pile. • Apply mulch to beds as needed. • Deadhead flowers. • Pick off caterpillars and beetles and discard in jar of soapy water.
WEDNESDAY	• Tie up straggling plants to stakes or cages. • Inspect all plants for insects (look under leaves and on new tip growth); if insect invasion is mild (little or no damage to plants observed) use plain water spray to dislodge insects. If leaves have been chewed or webbing and sticky residue is noticed, especially on backs of leaves, spray thoroughly with insecticidal soap. • Check for wilted squash leaves indicating borers; cut off affected stems.
THURSDAY	• If insect invasion was discovered, use soap spray again. • Cultivate soil around edges of containers and raised beds to reduce separation of soil from sides and loss of water. • Deadhead unsprayed plants. • Pick ripe vegetables and fruit. • Sift compost and sprinkle around base of plants. Record in notebook which beds and plants received compost.
FRIDAY	• Turn compost pile (every other week). Sift compost as needed and continue to spread around all plants. • Check stepping stones for level positioning; raise up if sinking. • Wash and oil tools as needed. • Cultivate compacted soil around base of plants.
SATURDAY	• Pick bouquets as flowers are available. • Deadhead flowers. • Water containers and raised beds if plants are beginning to wilt.
SUNDAY	• Weed containers. • Deadhead flowers. • Enjoy fragrance and texture with residents.

Controlling Creepy Crawlies and Plant Diseases Outdoors

Every healthy garden has insects. The trick is to balance the good with the bad, and to use all possible preventative measures to keep ahead of the pests. Good maintenance practices go hand in hand with the use of sprays. Organic methods will greatly reduce the bad bug population and will help produce healthier plants. Strict safety precautions when using any kind of spray or dust will protect people and other beneficial creatures that visit or live in the garden.

For Healthy Plants

- Choose an appropriate garden site that gets adequate sun and has well-drained soil.

- Buy healthy plants; plant healthy seedlings.

- Plant vegetables and flowers that are naturally resistant to insects and diseases or that have been hybridized to resist certain diseases. Read the catalog or seed packet information which describes the variety's resistance to wilt, mildew, scab, and other debilitating diseases.

- Keep weeds pulled.

- Discard all appropriate debris such as weeds, pinched flower heads, spent vegetable plants, discarded flower and houseplants, and fallen leaves in the compost pile. *Avoid adding* weed seed heads, any animal fat or meat from kitchen scraps, insect infested or diseased plants, and stems or sticks that are too thick to break down without using a chipper/shedder to the compost pile.

- Fertilize and mulch plants consistently.

- Water thoroughly, but don't overwater.

- Wait until water has evaporated from leaves before working in the garden.

- Dig finished composed from the bottom of the pile and sift it through a screen. Periodically apply the sifted compost to base of plants.

- Use companion planting for mutual benefits between appropriate plants.

To Control Insects

- Purchase an insect identification book, or print insect photos and descriptions from the Internet.

- Keep these commonly destructive insects in mind for identification: Aphids, spider mites, Japanese beetles, slugs, flea beetles, borers, caterpillars, cutworms, cucumber beetles, white flies.

- Keep these beneficial (helpful) insects in mind, and treat them with TLC: Ladybugs or lady beetles, lace wings, butterfly caterpillars (their benefit is enjoyed when they become butterflies!), parasitic wasps, honey bees, dragon flies, spiders, praying mantis.

- Burn or bag any garden debris containing eggs or obvious infestations of pest insects.

- Check under boards or other coverings where slugs can hide.

- Keep the garden beds and pathways free of debris where insects and slugs can hide.

- Try setting out saucers or pie pans of beer for slugs, or lay boards as slug traps. Use yellow painted "sticky" boards (coated with petroleum jelly) to attract flying insects.

- Cover vegetable crops with specialized netting constructed to keep insects out. Use foil or polystyrene collars around squash and tomato stems to discourage cutworms.

- Interplant insect repellent plants such as marigolds and basil with crops.

- Check leaves for insects and eggs (both topside and underneath) at least twice a week.

- Use a gentle, plain water spray on the undersides of leaves when watering to dislodge insects.

- Pick off caterpillars and larger insects such as Japanese beetles. Drop them into a pail of soapy water to drown them.

- Consider purchasing predator insects (e.g., ladybugs and parasitic wasps) if your population of destructive insects is high.

- Commercially prepared and registered insecticidal soap is effective against a number of soft-bodied insects. This type of spray does not harm bees, and is safe to use around both humans and animals.

As a last resort, use the **least toxic** types of manufactured organic or chemical insecticides after doing the following:

1. Identify the insect.
2. Try all the preceding methods, and research natural control methods.
3. Discuss it with the Plant Committee.
4. Use strict safety precautions when applying insecticides.

Choosing Appropriate Sprays and Dusts

Several choices of **manufactured organic pesticides** are available to control insects. Discuss the following with the Plant Committee members, gardening experts, and knowledgeable garden center personnel.

Fatty soap sprays are effective on a number of different types of insects. These sprays must be used according to directions, but have minimal harmful effects on humans or good wildlife.

Dusts and sprays made from natural ingredients such as pyrethrum, sabadilla, rotenone, and ryania can be effective, but in most cases are as toxic as chemical sprays. However, these can also cause violent allergic reactions in humans. They are *not* recommended for use where plants and people interact frequently.

Manufactured Dusts and Sprays for Mold, Mildew, and Fungus

These dusts are effective on the surface and not absorbed by the plant.

- *Microbial fungicides* reduce the spread of disease-producing organisms.
- *Garlic spray* seems to prevent some fungal organisms from developing.
- *Baking soda* can be sprayed on plants to prevent fungus.

- Sulfur and copper are very toxic and *must be used with caution.* A liquid, sulphur-based fungicide is available in stores.

Encouraging Resident Gardening Participation and Seasonal Awareness

Garden Club meetings provide the most consistent means of keeping residents informed of the garden's progress, and to motivate them to take part in the growing process. In addition to scheduled meetings, garden maintenance and guest speakers, many spontaneous interactions can take place at these gatherings.

Suggestions for keeping the residents and staff actively in tune with the season include:

- Encourage residents to take part in the Garden Club meetings and in the decision making process.
- Feature Garden Club members and their special gardening interests.
- Encourage residents to follow the progress of a certain plant from a seed or young transplant, to its maturity, and to report on the plant's progress at each weekly Garden Club meeting.
- Have tools and materials accessible for spontaneous use by residents, family and staff. If safe use of tools is an issue, keep the basics available at the nurses' station with a sign-out sheet. Hang a poster with a short list of gardening tasks to encourage residents and families to putter in the garden.

Garlic Spray

to treat mold, mildew, and fungus

> 5 large garlic cloves
> 1 pint water

Run five large garlic cloves and one pint of water through a blender. Strain through cheesecloth. Spray on plants that show signs of mildew or mold.

- Celebrate the first radish, tomato, rose bud or caterpillar sighting with a photo at the front desk.

- Bring in a trowel-full of partially finished compost to examine it with a magnifying glass.

- Include residents when picking flowers. Ask the resident to take the bouquet to a staff member or resident of his or her choice.

- When insects are observed, capture them (nonstinging type only). Bring them inside for observation.

- Post a flier with a gardening quote from the "Resident Gardener of the Week."

- Invite community garden club members to visit, present short topics, or demonstrate a craft.

- Call "emergency" Garden Club meetings to discuss what to do about a bug infestation or a sick plant.

Offer hands-on examination of seasonal changes:

- In spring, try the first flowers of spring, a branch showing new growth, force shrub branches to flower indoors, worms, a bird's nest in a sealed baggie, winter wheat sprouts, a cup of mud.

- In summer, tomato seedlings, warm compost, bean seeds, seed packets, garden tools, muddy boots, garden gloves, ripening fruit and vegetables, grass clippings.

- In fall, changing leaves, a bag of leaves, a rake, acorns, flower seed heads, bare branches.

Baking Soda Spray

to prevent fungus

   1 teaspoon baking soda
3–5 drops pure soap (Ivory or glycerin)
   2 quarts water

Mix baking soda and pure soap in warm water; allow to cool. Spray on plants to prevent fungus.

- In winter, a bowl of snow, frozen mud, dried ornamental grasses.

Involving Residents Who Are Moderately Confused or Have Limited Response

The same guidelines for indoor gardening apply to outdoor gardening as well with some differences depending on the number of residents involved and available volunteers. Some additional suggestions for outdoor activities that may be helpful include:

- Schedule a volunteer for small group activities.

- Hold the session outdoors in a quiet, shady area.

- Keep the group small (i.e., 4 or less).

- Provide sun hats when appropriate.

- Seat the residents around a card table or other easily transported table.

- Involve at least two participants in the same task (e.g., cultivating soil in a raised bed, picking out stones, cutting flowers, watering), so they can take cues from each other.

- Divide the session into a hands-on segment and a resting segment. For instance, first pot up a plant, then read a short story, poem, or other selection which is of interest to the reader.

- One-on-one sessions can involve all the senses—smell a fragrant flower, feel a fuzzy leaf, listen to a fountain, hold the hose while watering, watch a butterfly, listen to taped music, eat an organically grown pansy.

Children and Elders in the Garden

Individual outdoor gardening activities are featured in the Gardening Calendar with selected explanations. A few things to keep in mind:

- A comfortable place to sit or work is essential for the elders, convenient for the children, and aids organization of activities.

- Prevent accidents by keeping paths and patios clear of tools, hoses, and other equipment.

- A coordinated effort with children to help clean up and put away tools and supplies reduces cleanup time.

- Plan to wash muddy hands outdoors to make cleanup easier.

- Inform the newspaper about special children–elders gardening events to try to increase community interest, contributions, and volunteer ranks.

Harvesting for Fun, Profit, and Satisfaction

Almost any blossoming or fruiting crop will do better if it's picked slightly before maturity. This prevents seed formation, extends the blooming period of annuals and perennials, and encourages the plant to become fuller and produce more blooms. Harvesting vegetables as they ripen encourages the production of more vegetables and keeps the seed cavities smaller in some vegetables such as cucumbers and squash.

Some flower and herb harvesting pointers:

- For fresh table arrangements, cut the flowers with as long a stem as possible. Look for new shoots branching out from the notches between the flower stem and the main stalk. Cut above the new shoot, if possible. Place the flowers in a deep pail of warm water ASAP. Arrange in a vase of cold water.

- Cut as early in the day as possible.

- Wash herbs to be used for food seasoning. Pat dry in clean terry towels or paper towels.

- When cutting flowers for drying, make sure the dew has dried, and choose half-opened blooms. Don't pick damaged or infested flowers. Cut the stems at different lengths. Strip off the lower leaves, arrange the ends of the stems together, and fasten with a rubber band. Hang upside down in a room with good air circulation and out of direct sunlight. Stretch a lightweight chain or knotted rope across a room and hang the

bundles of flowers from it—this way they won't slide into each other.

- Give flowers and herbs time to dry (usually one to three weeks). They should feel light and stiff when dry—not limp and leathery.

- Flower heads or petals may be dried on window screens or newspaper.

- When herbs are thoroughly dry and crispy, strip the leaves from stems, and place them in airtight containers. Label with name and date, and store.

- Some effective, color-retaining but more time-consuming and labor-intensive methods to preserve flower heads is by covering them with various combinations of sand, oatmeal, borax, silica gel, or oolitic sand. For more details about these methods, see Clemson University's Extension Fact Sheet entitled *Drying Flowers* (Pertuit, 2002; see *References and resources*, p. 134).

- Store dried material in a dark closet or drawer, paper bags, boxes, or in airtight containers.

Several herbs are attractive when cut and pressed in a heavy book and later used in Christmas cards or sent in cellophane packages with greeting cards. These include: thyme, rosemary, pennyroyal, and costmary. Short descriptions and meanings of each herb make unique gifts. Lamb's ear leaves can be pressed and used as bookmarks.

Usually some staff members will have access to grapevines. Ask for lengths of vine to make different sized wreaths. Pick a variety of herbs and flowers and decorate the wreaths while the materials are still fresh and pliable. The fuller the wreath, the more attractive the finished product will be. Fresh materials shrink as they dry.

Putting the Outdoor Garden to Bed for the Winter

A few simple chores will reduce next year's springtime maintenance and improve the soil's texture and nutritional value. Call in your volunteers an afternoon cleanup session in mid to late October (or even later depending on the climate), and then throw a pizza party to thank them. Facilities in warmer climates with a longer growing season will need to keep these valuable people occupied with additional cooler season crops, or renewing tired flower beds and vegetable crops. When cleaning up the garden, the following checklist may be helpful:

❑ Ask residents for their cleanup suggestions. Make a list, and post it.

❑ Continue to water perennials as needed up to the first frost.

❑ If fall crops were planted, row cover (i.e., a synthetic lightweight material which allows air, sunlight and water to penetrate while protecting crops from frost, wind chill and insects) may be needed.

Annual Flower and Vegetable Disposal

❑ Pull up the finished annual crops, vines, and flowers (including the root balls). Shake off the soil, and add them to compost pile.

❑ Rake all leaf, stem, flower, and produce debris. Add it to the compost pile.

❑ Ideally, run all large chunks and pieces of debris through a chipper/shredder. Break and/or chop all large debris into small pieces appropriate for the compost pile with a sharp shovel if you don't have a shredder.

❑ Clean out raised beds and containers in the same manner. Cultivate the soil as deeply as possible.

Compost Pile Care and Use

❑ Thoroughly mix the pile.

❑ Make a shallow depression in the top of the pile to collect rainwater. Water the pile occasionally when the weather is dry.

❑ If sufficient half-finished (partially decomposed, but still having chunks of material) compost is available, spread it over the surface of the ground beds to finish decomposing over the winter. Otherwise, use clean straw or shredded leaves.

Raised Beds and Containers

❑ Cover the soil of the raised beds and large containers with clean straw, shredded leaves, or grass clippings that haven't been sprayed with chemicals.

❑ Empty and store all small containers and pots (especially those made of clay) to prevent cracking from freezing and thawing over the winter.

Perennials and Shrubs

❑ Leave perennial flower seed heads such as cone flower, sedum "live forever," staghorn sumac and ornamental grasses for bird forage and winter visual interest.

❑ Trim dead foliage plants to promote fresh growth in spring (e.g., chives, thyme, butterfly bush, day lilies).

❑ Wait until spring to trim roses, clematis and other woody perennials and shrubs such as mock orange and hydrangeas to avoid cutting potential bud growth.

Green Manure

❑ Ask your Master Gardener about sowing *green manure crops*. These are crops grown for a short period and then tilled into the soil to add organic material and nutrients. *Clover* can be sown in late summer or fall, and its growth tilled into the soil three to four weeks before planting the garden bed in spring. *Winter rye* can be sown in late summer or fall, and tilled into the bed in spring as well. Be sure the areas to be planted with green manure crops are well-drained to avoid tilling wet soil in the spring.

Additional things to do during the sunny days of October and crisp days of November:

❑ Inspect perennial shrubs and fruit trees for scale insects, and spray while these insects are dormant.

❑ Watch for aphids and white flies on late flowering perennials and treat as needed.

❑ Ask residents to listen to weather reports for frost. Cover tender garden plants with sheets supported by stakes or synthetic row cover material to protect them.

❑ If space is available, pull tomato vines before the first frost and hang them in a garage, barn or shed to ripen, or wrap individual green tomatoes in newspaper and place them in a cardboard box in a basement or other above-freezing area.

❑ In November, plant dwarf fruit trees and shrubs.

❑ Dig up any tender (i.e., nonhardy) tubers or bulbs, shake off dirt, and store them in shredded newspaper, sawdust, sand, or peat moss in a cool, dry area.

❑ Take cuttings from geraniums, herbs, begonias, and any other potential houseplant. Let the cut ends dry overnight, then dip the ends in rooting hormone before setting in pots of sterile soil to root.

❑ In warmer climates, protect late crops such as raspberries and lingonberries from hungry birds by covering them with row covers. This will also extend the growing season by reducing light frost damage.

Volunteers from youth programs and garden clubs would be good candidates for these tasks:

❑ Repair any rough or splintered edges on raised beds. Discard broken or cracked containers.

❑ Hang restored or new bird feeders.

❑ Hang sunflower heads or husk seeds from flower heads for use in feeders.

❑ Decide on squirrel feeding issue. Place squirrel feeders as needed.

❑ Inspect fencing or edging for breaks.

❑ Patch and repair pathways.

❑ Have a tool cleanup session with residents. Sand off rust, oil metal and wooden parts; sharpen edges as needed.

❑ If rabbits may be a problem, wrap the trunks of young trees.

❑ Turn off the water. Drain and store the hoses.

❑ Empty and store pottery containers to prevent cracking from ice buildup.

❑ Discuss planting spring bulbs with reference to their being toxic. Can they be planted without risk to pets, but within residents' visual enjoyment?

❑ *Continue to keep volunteer and family interest through newsletter mailings and direct distribution.*

Part 4: Nurturing and Keeping the Growing Spirit

Seasons come and go, and in an energetic garden environment, the expectation of new growth continues. Even as the garden is put to bed, plans are being made for next year's flowers and vegetables, and cuttings from this year's herbs are being taken. During the winter months, residents and staff discuss their garden successes and disappointments and look forward to experiencing improved methods and new varieties.

Continuing Plant Committee Interest

As the seasonal holidays approach and everyone becomes wrapped up in personal preparation for these celebrations, it's important to make the best use of staff and volunteer time and energy. The Plant Committee must effectively communicate with the Plant Team and the Garden Team, the Activities department and volunteers in order to keep all participants actively (but realistically) involved. Plan meetings and content to include:

- Flyers/letters to Plant Committee, Plant Team, and Garden Team members with a brief description of the meetings' purpose, indicating that the meeting will be "short and sweet," but important. Include a brief agenda.

- Consider skipping the December meeting, but instead send holiday cards to the members. Include a group photo in a garden theme border mat. These can be purchased inexpensively and decorated by Garden Club residents.

- Discuss seasonal issues such as displaying information on "Safe plants for gift giving," "Garden supplies needed for spring," or "Join us for a holiday tour of the City Botanical Garden."

- Set the date for the January meeting. Briefly describe the need for current seed catalogs, new crop ideas, and a refresher course in seed starting.

Recordkeeping

The method and style of keeping an outdoor garden log can be based on the way in which you chose to do the indoor plant log. This log should be in its own binder and can include:

- A simple diagram of the garden layout.

- What crops were planted outdoors and when.

- Plant problems and how they were treated.

- Separate sheets for volunteers, their time in the garden, and/or their involvement in other gardening activities.

- List of community people or places to call for gardening assistance.

- Where how-to reference books are located.

- Routine weekly garden task sheets.

- Safety precautions and personnel to contact in case of emergencies.

- The Garden Team schedule.

Building a Reference Library

By now, the indoor and outdoor gardening library should have a shelf of its own. If this has not happened, review the ways and means of collecting good reference books. Set up a method for funding books and ask for donations. Ask Master Gardeners and other reliable people for a list of publications with clear and accurate guidelines and information (or start with the *Resources*, pp. 131–136).

Turning Dreams into Reality

Take time to evaluate the actual needs for the gardening effort as compared to the wishes of the residents, staff, and volunteers. A successful program must contain at least these basics:

- Tools, equipment, and a core group of staff and volunteers

- Ideas or perspectives gained from visiting other residential garden programs. Plan a field trip to facilities with established gardening programs in place to swap ideas.

- Resident interest, comfort, and satisfaction.

- Communication with and support from the administration.

There is never really an end to the gardening cycle, but this time of year brings a lull in the needs of the garden plants and a welcome respite for the gardeners. This might be a time of reminiscing for many residents, as they recall their childhood on the farm or how they enjoyed their mothers' home canned beans, tomatoes, and sauerkraut. The support and efforts of the staff reinforce these precious memories. In the upcoming New Year, the residents and staff will continue to prepare the ground and lay the groundwork for future seasons.

The Gardening Calendar

This monthly calendar contains a variety of guidelines for indoor and outdoor gardening approaches, garden group meetings, spontaneous interactions, and activities with children for an entire year. References and selected explanations are included.

The Plant and Garden Teams, residents, and volunteers from each of the Home's neighborhoods might want to meet together periodically to compare notes and plan activities. Resources can be combined and certain materials shared such as books, specialty or exotic plants, an ant or worm farm, a seeding device, children's tools, texture samples, and aroma materials.

The indoor and outdoor plant care sections are based on seasonal tasks which will vary according to climate zones. Items such as "resident personal plant care," "weekly public plant care," or "outdoor garden care" along with special gardening events such as an "Herb tea party" or "Bonsai speaker" can be listed in the general resident activity calendar or posted on an independent gardening calendar. Integrating these tasks into the general calendar will gradually accustom everyone to the routines of the greenery and the gardening aspect of the Human Habitat.

The Potpourri section contains "Items for the Month" that can be adapted to any group, including residents with dementia, those benefiting from sensory stimulation, children, and Garden Club participants. Selected explanations are included with references for further reading and expansion.

The Plant and Garden Teams or Activities personnel are encouraged to research meaningful ethnic and religious holidays where the use of herbs or other plants is traditional. This can then be the basis for food preparation and discussions.

The Internet contains many excellent gardening and wildlife references and how-to activities. Consider scheduling time with a computer-oriented staff member, resident, or volunteer to locate online references and resources.

January

Indoor Plant Care

Daily

- ❏ Spot-check for trash in flower pots.
- ❏ Walk by plant areas; observe plants for wilting.
- ❏ Observe for standing water in saucers.
- ❏ Check seed trays and new seedlings for consistent moisture.
- ❏ Be aware of significant temperature changes in plant environments.

Weekly

- ❏ Resident personal plant care.
- ❏ Public areas/Neighborhood plant care.
- ❏ Clean and restock plant cart.
- ❏ Check cuttings in water for roots; check cuttings in soil for appropriate moisture.
- ❏ Transplant seedlings as they develop their first or second set of true leaves.

Monthly

- ❏ Observe for effect of light exposure (e.g., even growth, sunburned, spindly); rearrange plants needing a different light exposure.
- ❏ Cultivate soil as needed; add mulch.
- ❏ Post "Plant of the Month" information.
- ❏ Post the Plant Team(s) schedule.
- ❏ Check volunteer sheets.
- ❏ Hold Plant Team and volunteer (including resident volunteers) meeting.
- ❏ Post the gardening calendar (if separate), or submit gardening events to be included in general activities calendar.
- ❏ As appropriate, include article about indoor plants in the facility newsletter.
- ❏ Submit a newsworthy article to the local media (e.g., newspaper, radio station).

Outdoor Garden Care

Daily

- ❏ Observe the shape and form of bare trees and shrubs.
- ❏ Check wildlife water supply; consider a heating element if the water freezes.
- ❏ Refill bird and squirrel feeders. Ask residents to report empty feeders.
- ❏ Observe the varieties of birds at the feeder and discuss them. A resident may want to keep track of sightings.
- ❏ Collect banana peels, apple cores, and, if appropriate, kitchen vegetable scraps for the compost pile; add to compost pile daily.
- ❏ Have garden seed catalogs available for residents, staff, and family to read.

Weekly

- ❏ Depending on the climate and the condition of the soil, till or turn the garden beds to expose buried insect eggs to the elements and hungry birds.
- ❏ Observe shadow patterns at this time of year. What part of the garden is in full shade? Where is it sunny?
- ❏ In warmer climates, maintain and use winter crops.
- ❏ Start to mix soilless recipe, or buy mix for seed starting.
- ❏ Begin to record resident and staff requests for crops (see *Garden Club Meeting Ideas*).
- ❏ Include bird-attracting shrubs and trees in the plan for garden plants.
- ❏ Check tool condition; sharpen and/or oil as needed.
- ❏ Start saving small milk cartons for seedling transplants. Open cartons and rinse thoroughly; turn up-side-down to dry. Poke holes in the bottom of the cartons. Store for later use.

Monthly

- ❑ Pick up sticks and larger garden debris.
- ❑ Transplant herb cuttings to next sized pot.
- ❑ Check condition of seed-starting shelf lights, containers/flats, and so forth.
- ❑ Buy a timer or have one donated for the fluorescent lights.

Potpourri

Texture: Various kinds of tree bark. Ask a local youth group to gather the bark.

Herb: Caraway (*Carum carvi*)

Houseplant: Strawberry begonia. Propagate by pinning several plantlets to the surface of potting mix in separate container from the mother plant. Pin down with hairpins or paper clips, making certain underside of plantlet comes in contact with soil. Cover with a plastic bag. Do not cut the stems to the mother plant until roots form on the baby plantlets.

Flower: Gardenia. Ask a local florist or greenhouse for a plant or cut flowers. Gardenias are a tricky plant to grow, but worth the effort. Check houseplant reference books or search the Internet using the keyword "gardenia."

Tree: Corkscrew willow (*Salix matsudana tortuosa*; zones 5–9). Branches might be found in a floral arrangement or ask local grower for several young cuttings. Place in water in bright light until roots form. Pot up in mixture of half soilless mix and half compost. Plant outside as soon as the soil warms.

Wildlife: Squirrel. Find information to share at the library, through the Department of Natural Resources, the Extension Service, or on the Internet.

Garden Club Meeting Ideas

- Discuss and make a chart of resident, staff, and others' requests for garden crops.
- Invite a local Master Gardener to give a talk about flower and vegetable varieties for that year.

- Review last year's garden sketch. Add new crops, raised beds, and paths to the sketch as needed.
- Decide on new structures such as a cold frame, trellises, arbors, and other garden accents.
- When decisions are made about crops, order seeds from catalogs or purchase them locally. Make a poster from catalog cutouts.
- Have residents mix soil for seed starting or fill containers or cell packs with purchased mix to prepare for planting seeds. Stack on seed-starting shelves until needed. When it's time to moisten the flats of soil, place them in a larger tray and bottom water.
- Invite an Herb Club member to assist in planning a small herb garden.
- Make and serve an herb snack.
- **Book of the Month:** Jenkins, E. (1993). *Pleasure of the garden.* New York, NY: Crown.

Spontaneous Interactions

- Point out the species of birds at the feeders.

- Ask a resident what the outside temperature is, or for the weather report that day.

- Point out new blooms on flowering plants, newly opening leaves on foliage plants, roots forming on cuttings in water, or 'baby' begonias sprouting by vein-cutting method (see *Growing and propagating houseplants*, p. 45).

- Celebrate when seeds sprout and 'true' leaves form.

- Spread the word when the cat eats some catnip or the grass grown especially for it.

Having Fun With Kids

- Use discarded Christmas trees in the garden for bird and wildlife cover.

- Tie yarn to pine cones. Fill the crevices with peanut butter and roll them in birdseed. Hang on the Christmas trees outside.

- Make a collage illustrating wildlife in the winter garden.

- Hold a show-and-tell with tree bark samples from several different trees.

- **Book:** Reed-Jones, C. (1995). *The tree in the ancient forest*. Nevada City, CA: Dawn Publications.

February

Indoor Plant Care

Daily

- ❏ Spot-check for trash in flower pots.
- ❏ Observe plants for wilting.
- ❏ Observe for standing water in saucers.
- ❏ Check seed trays for new seedlings and consistent moisture.
- ❏ Be aware of significant temperature changes in plant environments.

Weekly

- ❏ Resume diluted fertilizing toward the end of month as daylight lengthens.
- ❏ Try using Knox unflavored gelatin as a nitrogen boost on a few small plants and watch for changes. Mix one envelope of Knox gelatin with one cup hot tap water to dissolve. Slowly add three cups of warm water. Let cool. Use this in place of normal water once a month.
- ❏ Resident personal plant care.
- ❏ Neighborhood plant care.
- ❏ Restock and clean plant cart.
- ❏ Check cuttings.
- ❏ Transplant seedlings as true leaves develop.
- ❏ Prepare light shelves for seed starting.

Monthly

- ❏ Days are getting longer. Observe for effect of light exposure; rearrange plants as needed.
- ❏ Cultivate soil; add mulch.
- ❏ Have the cats been using the pots as litter boxes?
- ❏ Post "Plant of the Month" information.
- ❏ Post Plant Team(s) schedule.
- ❏ Check volunteer sheets.
- ❏ Hold Plant and Garden Team, Resident and Volunteer meeting.

- ❏ Consider arranging a tour of the indoor gardens for administration and board members.
- ❏ Post the gardening calendar or submit gardening events to the general calendar editor.
- ❏ Submit an article to the facility newsletter.
- ❏ Post an update about gardening activities at the front desk.

Outdoor Garden Care

Daily

- ❏ Feed birds and squirrels; refill feeders and water.
- ❏ Observe for returning species of birds; record sightings.
- ❏ Collect vegetable and fruit scraps for compost; turn and mix compost thoroughly.
- ❏ Remind residents and staff to finalize their garden crop choices.

❏ Place seed catalog orders.

❏ Know your region's USDA plant hardiness zone. Call the Extension Service to be sure.

Weekly

❏ Review *Starting seeds indoors* (p. 72).

❏ Prepare materials for seed starting: Seed starting mix, flats or containers for soil, plastic labels, seed starting list, a spray water bottle.

❏ Check operation of light timer.

❏ Start perennial flower seeds and early vegetable seeds under the lights.

❏ Plant early leaf crops and peas outdoors in warmer areas. Harvest root crops which wintered over in the beds; harvest perennials such as rhubarb and asparagus if ready.

❏ Plant dormant fruit trees.

❏ Prune fruit trees, berry canes, and grape vines.

❏ Spray fruit trees with oil emulsion for scale insects. Check with a Master Gardener or the County Extension Office for proper timing of applying oil.

❏ Decide on the need for buying or building garden structures such as a cold frame, raised beds, birdhouses, arbors, and trellises. Who will be responsible for the cost and construction? What volunteer agencies or individuals will help?

❏ Check tools. Clean, oil, and sharpen as needed. Is there appropriate storage for tools outside?

Monthly

❏ Clean up garden debris.

❏ Decide on members of Garden Team. Are volunteers lined up?

❏ Post the Garden Team(s) schedule.

❏ Organize a Garden Care Log with routine task sheets, and volunteer schedules and hours (see *Recordkeeping*, p. 95).

Potpourri

Texture: Feathers (all kinds)

Herb: Oregano. A good herb book from the library or *The Rodale Herb Book* (Hylton, 1974) will provide information about this herb. Make mini-pizzas using English muffins, tomato sauce, mozzarella and parmesan cheeses, and oregano. Bake at 350°F approximately 5 minutes or until the cheese melts.

Houseplant: Sensitive plant (*Mimosa pudica*). Can be ordered from Park's Seed Company or Thompson and Morgan. Place seeds between fine sandpaper and sand lightly to remove outside shell. Soak overnight before planting.

Flower: Cotton (*Gossypium hirsutum*). Annual in zones 5–7 where it needs to be started inside for a growing season of 150 days. In zones 8–10 it can be sown directly into the garden after the last frost. Order now to give the seeds an early start.

Tree: White birch (*Betula papyrifer*; also known as paper birch or canoe birch). Grows in zones 2–10.

Wildlife: Ladybug. Any good insect book; a catalog of beneficial insects is available from The Bug Store, 800–455–2847.

Garden Club Meeting Ideas

• Seed-starting sessions that include children.

• If appropriate, ask resident volunteers to monitor seed trays for sprouting plants, and for watering needs.

• Complete a current sketch of all resident gardens.

• Share information pertinent to Neighborhood gardens with residents.

• Hold a mini in-service about watering seedlings.

• Discuss perennial crops such as rhubarb, artichokes, horseradish, and asparagus.

• **Speaker**: An occupational therapist or tool company representative speaking about adaptive (easy and comfortable) gardening tools, and how to use them properly.

- **Book of the Month:** Kramer, J. (1999). *Easy-care guide to houseplants*. Upper Saddle River, NJ: Creative Homeowner.

Spontaneous Interactions

- Report any insects. Ask residents to be on the lookout for insect invasions, and plants becoming "sunburned."
- Remark on the returning birds.
- What's happening in the compost pile?
- Any new seedlings sprouting?
- Pick up a seed catalog or *Farmer's Almanac* and look through it with a resident.
- Discuss rhubarb pie, how to cook asparagus, and how to handle an artichoke.
- Observe and discuss late winter and early spring blooms.

Having Fun With Kids

- Locate spring flowering shrubs and observe for buds. These can be cut later in the month, or in March to bring inside to bloom (e.g., forsythia, flowering quince, flowering plum, dogwood tree).
- Make feathers with construction paper. Ask a Cub scout or Brownie troop to collect real feathers. Draw a large imaginary bird on posterboard and decorate it with feathers, leaves, pieces of pinecones, fungus, acorns, and anything else available from nature.
- Plant sensitive plant seeds (*Mimosa pudica*).
- Discuss growing cotton.
- **Book:** Stewart, S. (1997). *The gardener*. New York, NY: Farrar, Straus, Giroux.

March

At this point, the indoor and outdoor care begin to "run into each other" as the planting and care of seedlings increases. The secret is to be conservative about the amount of seeds to start for outdoor growing. Starting small for the experience will bring greater success than choosing many varieties and having a too many plants. Once the indoor seed-starting routine is in place, greater numbers and kinds of plants can be tried the next year. Know the **frost date** for your area.

Indoor Plant Care

Daily

❏ Days are getting longer—Observe for new growth.

❏ Observe how emerging leaves on the trees outside are casting shadows inside.

❏ Consider how to rearrange the houseplants that have been stored on the light shelves since seedlings will now be grown there.

Weekly

❏ Resident personal plant care.

❏ Neighborhood plant care.

❏ Restock and clean plant cart.

❏ Transplant rooted cuttings as needed.

❏ Transplant seedlings as needed.

❏ Find safe locations for any toxic gift plants that were brought to residents.

❏ Take cuttings for an in-house exchange or "winter clearance" sale. Cuttings can be taken the day of sale and placed in water, then in plastic bags for customers. Alternatively, cuttings can be taken, rooted and potted up in 3-inch pots to sell. Evaluate method according to the number of cuttings and space available.

❏ Rearrange work space to accommodate transplanting outdoor garden seedlings.

❏ Collect empty milk cartons. Wash, poke holes in bottom, and save for transplanting seedlings.

Monthly

❏ Transplant larger potbound houseplants. Signs of being potbound include: roots are showing above the soil or protruding from drainage holes; soil is drying out resulting in more frequent watering needs. **Don't repot plants that need to be potbound to bloom** such as night-blooming cereus or spider plants.

❏ Send out fliers announcing a plant sale.

❏ Evaluate location of plants for light exposure.

❏ Post Plant Team schedule, plant of the month, and gardening calendar.

❏ Hold an exchange or sale.

❏ Meet with Home's Plant and Garden Team(s) and volunteers.

Outdoor Garden Care

Daily

❏ Review *Starting seeds indoors* (p. 72).

❏ Calculate when to start seeds according to package directions and amount of space to locate growing seedlings. Don't start too early and be sure to have alternate place for seedlings after they outgrow the seed starting shelves (e.g., south-facing window, cold frame).

❏ Write the seed name and date started on plastic labels and stick in each seed cell pack.

❏ Ask resident volunteers to help watch for sprouting seeds and seedling watering needs.

Weekly

❏ Watch the height of growing seedlings—Are they getting too close to the fluorescent lights?

❏ Monitor watering needs of seedlings (especially if using peat pellets).

❏ As seeds sprout and while seedlings are still small, use a spray bottle to water them to prevent overwatering.

❏ Prevent overcrowding by transplanting seedlings into separate pots or thinning them with small scissors by cutting some at soil level. Don't pull out seedlings—this can damage the neighboring seedling's roots.

❑ When seedlings have their first or second true set of leaves, transplant them to individual containers with soil containing dry fertilizer.

❑ Outside in the garden, rake back the mulch to allow soil to dry.

❑ Spade or till the garden beds and planters if this wasn't done in the fall.

❑ Plant early salad greens, peas, vegetables plants, and some early flowers such as sweet peas, alyssum, and dianthus (pinks).

❑ Watch for sprouting perennial vegetables and flowers.

❑ Continue to feed the birds.

Monthly

❑ Orient volunteers to garden plans. Will there be enough volunteers on a regular basis?

❑ Will volunteers assist with transplanting?

❑ Are birdhouses in place?

❑ Contact local Garden Clubs' about donating plants that attract wildlife. Will the clubs be responsible for planting also?

❑ On a sunny day, take some residents and children out to turn the compost pile.

❑ Discuss how to control wildlife pests (e.g., rabbits, chipmunks, moles). Call the Department of Natural Resources.

❑ Post the Garden Team schedule. Include "Outdoor Garden Maintenance" on the calendar.

❑ Write a short update for the newsletter about garden progress.

Potpourri

Texture: Bird's nest materials (e.g., dried grass, yarn, string, moss, lichen)

Herb: Dandelion. See *The Rodale Herb Book* (Hylton, 1974).

Houseplant: Rabbit's foot fern (*Davallia*). Call local greenhouses to locate one.

Tree: Bonsai (any kind). These are miniature versions of many species of trees. Many can be grown inside. Some need wintering in a protected spot outside. Ask Master Gardeners if they know of a local expert, or find a greenhouse employee who would give a short demonstration about bonsai.

Flower: Your state flower (call your Department of Natural Resources).

Wildlife: Your state bird (call your Department of Natural Resources)

Garden Club Meeting Ideas

• Update about seeds planted, seedlings, seeds to be started, and the garden plans.

• Discuss the dandelion and demonstrate its uses.

• **Speaker:** Discuss and decide about plants to attract hummingbirds.

• Clean, oil, and wax tools.

• Make a potato planter out of several tires, a whiskey barrel, or purchase one from a catalog.

- Decide how to label plants and vegetables. Make markers.

- Make and serve herb bread. Borrow a breadmaker for the best aroma; use dried herbs.

- **Book of the Month:** Schultz, W. (1998). *For your garden: Vines and climbers*. New York, NY: Barnes and Noble.

Spontaneous Interactions

- Share a new library book, flower, or wildlife magazine.

- Play garden songs or environmental music.

- Remove seedling trays and show them to resident and family member.

- Sniff an herb with a resident. Rub the leaves or pinch off a few.

- Take a resident outside to pick up sticks for starting or adding to a wildlife brush pile.

Having Fun with Kids

- Plant zinnia seeds to attract butterflies (see seed packet directions for planting time). Use peat pellets for easy handling. Don't let the pellets dry out.

- Consider a small raised bed for "kids' crops." Try radishes, nasturtiums, mini-carrots, silver dollar plant (*Lunaria*), lemon basil, lamb's ear (*Stachys lanata*), dwarf zinnias, dwarf sunflowers, pincushion plant "Ping Pong," and Easter eggplant (can be found in Park's Seed Catalog).

- Start parsley seeds outdoors for caterpillar food. Parsley plants get large, so plan accordingly.

- Make "toad abodes" using old or cracked pottery pots. Break off a section of the rim to make a doorway, and set the pot upside down in a sheltered garden spot. Sink a dish into the soil nearby, fill it with water and a rock.

- Hang a potato sack (with widely spaced mesh) on a low tree branch or in a protected location where residents can view it from a window. Place bird nesting material in the sack (e.g., pieces of yarn, dryer lint, dried grass, moss, feathers, string, thin strips of newspaper).

- **Book:** Slepian, J. (1995). *Lost moose*. New York, NY: Philomel Books.

April

The amount and intensity of natural light is increasing. Check houseplants in southern and western windows for sunburn. A Mother's Day plant sale will bring in some cash from the rooted cuttings and extra seedlings beginning to sprout. As plans for the garden take shape, resident and staff interest will become more focused. Ask for donations of small plastic flowerpots for transplants. Weeds will be rearing their nasty heads and need to be identified. Warm days will invite more outdoor activity. Continue to listen for frost warnings.

Indoor Plant Care

Daily

- ❏ Maintain usual observance of trash removal, dry and wet soil, too much or too little light.
- ❏ Spot-check for insect invasions.
- ❏ Be alert for ragged, chewed-on leaf ends which can indicate that the cats are looking for tasty greenery or a new toy.
- ❏ Consider a Mother's Day plant sale using potted houseplant cuttings and extra seedlings of annuals and herbs.

Weekly

- ❏ Purchase or ask for donations of herb plants and cuttings.
- ❏ Place herbs in the sunniest windows.
- ❏ Resident personal plant care.
- ❏ Neighborhood plant care.
- ❏ Restock and clean plant cart.
- ❏ Transplant cuttings as needed.
- ❏ Get plants ready for Mother's Day sale.

Monthly

- ❏ Routine fertilization. Remember to use half as much fertilizer, half as often.
- ❏ Cultivate soil and add mulch as needed.
- ❏ Post plant of the month information, Plant Team schedule, Plant Team and Volunteer meeting agenda, and the gardening calendar.

- ❏ Write an article or update for the newsletter.
- ❏ Prepare fliers for the Mother's Day plant sale.

Outdoor Garden Care

Daily

- ❏ Residents can help look for sprouting weeds and pull them while they are still small.
- ❏ Watch for birds' nests and young birds.
- ❏ Keep a close eye on seedlings and transplants.
- ❏ If cold frame is to be used, plan where and when to set it up.
- ❏ Early in month, cut flowering shrub and tree branches for forced blooming inside.
- ❏ Deadhead or cut back perennials. Removing spent (old) blooms before they begin to go to seed will extend the blooming time of plants. Chives can be cut back to 4–6 inches high before the blooms begin to dry and go to seed, and chives will rebloom in a few weeks. Not all perennials respond this way, but by

keeping the plant from putting its energy into seed formation, its blooming life will be extended.

Weekly

❑ Start seeds inside as directed.

❑ Watch for and pull weeds in garden beds.

❑ Snip salad greens; pull early radishes.

❑ Plant hardy annual flower seeds directly into garden beds since these can withstand cool nights; check seed packet (e.g., sweet peas, alyssum, candytuft, pot marigold, larkspur, annual poppies).

❑ Plant several small lavender plants. Use varieties hardy to your area to form a stand of lavender for a good supply of blooms. Space according to seed packet directions.

❑ Planting seeds directly into garden beds saves time. Soil in seed beds should be loose. Add a layer of seed-starting mix for easy sprouting. Scatter seeds or space them to avoid transplanting; cover as directed, then spread with light straw or grass mulch to protect the seeds from birds or from being washed away by rain. Keep these beds moist until seeds sprout.

Monthly

❑ Turn compost pile.

❑ Post Garden Team schedule.

❑ Have all outdoor garden tools ready for use.

❑ Have a safe tool and fertilizer storage method in place.

❑ Invite management personnel to visit the garden with resident tour guides.

❑ Decide on need for an outdoor plant cart or other means for staff and residents to carry tools, the notebook, and other supplies.

Potpourri

Texture: Half-finished compost

Herb: Parsley

Houseplant: Mosaic plant (*Fittonia*)

Tree: Dogwood (*Cornus florida*; zones 5–9)

Flower: Masterwort (*Astrantia major* Primadona; perennial in zones 4–7)

Wildlife: Butterfly. Look for Brooklyn Botanic Garden's *Butterfly Gardens* (Lewis, 1995).

Garden Club Meetings

• Update about outdoor garden progress.

• Organize and prepare plants for May Mother's Day plant sale.

• Maintain potato planter.

• Do residents want a birdbath? Who will fill and clean it?

• **Reading:** Current issue of *Horticulture*, *Organic Gardening*, or *Country* magazines.

• Make herb butter and serve on crackers. Mince fresh herbs (e.g., chives, parsley, oregano, cilantro). Mix thoroughly with tub margarine or softened butter. Let sit overnight in refrigerator to blend flavors. Spread on crackers.

Spontaneous Interactions

• **Music:** "April Showers," "Inch by Inch," selections from *Appalachian Spring*.

• Ask a resident to help with transplanting for ten minutes.

• Take a resident outside to discover seeds sprouting, or for a five-minute weeding session.

• Point out new leaves on seedlings and the beginning of buds.

• Share an article in a gardening magazine or read a spring poem.

Having Fun with Kids

• Teach children the song "Inch by Inch" by David Mallett as found in *The John Denver Anthology* songbook.

• Plant seeds of annual vines such as black-eyed Susan vine, nasturtiums, and canary bird flower. **Caution:** Some annual vine seeds are **toxic** including morning glory, moon flower vine, and sweet peas. If toxic types are to be sown, their location should be out of the reach of any residents or children.

- Bring in a shovelful of half-finished compost. Examine all the fascinating creatures working together. Use a magnifying glass.

- Plant all varieties of sunflowers directly into garden beds.

- Study the honey bee.

- **Book:** Maass, R. (1994). *When spring comes.* New York, NY: Henry Holt and Co.

May

Houseplants can be moved outside to reduce crowding and increase indoor seating space. Find a semishaded spot for the tender tropicals, and check periodically for evidence of sunburn. Be sure to leave a few interesting plants inside for resident and visitor enjoyment. Where will the seedlings be hardened off before planting? A cold frame may be the answer. Keep brief but accurate records of seed starting and garden care to save time and labor in the future.

Indoor Plant Care

Daily

❏ Monitor changing light exposure inside and its effect on houseplants.

❏ Transplant seedlings and rooted cuttings.

Weekly

❏ If space is needed inside, ficus trees and other large floor plants can be moved outside to brighter light but not full sun. These plants may need watering more often when outside.

❏ Resident personal plant care. When the nights warm up, residents may want to put their plants outdoors. Is there an appropriate spot for the plants? Do they want to risk outdoor insect infestation?

❏ Public plant care. Restock and clean the plant cart.

❏ Post fliers for the Mother's Day plant sale.

❏ Gather plants for the Mother's Day sale. Check for correct labels. Organize staff, time, space, and accessories for sale.

Monthly

❏ Post Plant of the Month information.

❏ Schedule Plant Team(s). Include gardening events on the calendar. Hold a Plant Team meeting to update and motivate members.

❏ Fertilize houseplants.

❏ Cut back (prune) overgrown or leggy houseplants to approximately half their height.

Outdoor Garden Care

Daily

❏ Discuss continuing to feed the birds during the summer.

❏ Begin deadheading old blossoms on garden annuals. Using scissors rather than pinching might be faster.

Weekly

❏ Begin to harden off transplanted seedlings in a cold frame or outside in a protected garden spot. Gradually move them to a more open exposure prior to planting in ground.

❏ Take time to sit and enjoy the warmth and life in the garden.

Monthly

❏ Prepare the garden bed rows where vegetable and flower transplants are to be placed by adding bone meal and blood meal in appropriate amounts, or by sifting finished compost into a container and having it ready to mix in each planting hole. In the interest of time and labor, chemical fertilizers may be used, but be sure to incorporate a generous amount of compost as it becomes available.

❏ After the last frost date, begin to place transplants into beds. Refer to seed packet instructions for **spacing** plants, and to your garden plan for locating plants.

❏ Mulch after planting. Use straw for vegetables and available materials for flowers (e.g., shredded hardwood, cocoa bean hulls).

❏ Set tomato cages and plant stakes as the plants are placed into the garden.

❏ Schedule Garden Team(s). Include gardening events on the calendar. Hold a Team meeting to update and motivate members.

❏ Record when various vegetables are harvested, when flowers bloom, and when bird species come and go.

❑ Is fencing needed to deter rabbits, deer or other wildlife?

❑ Update the Neighborhood Team on garden happenings, and how anyone on the Team can help with garden care.

❑ Encourage residents, visitors, and staff to assist with garden tasks at their convenience. Place a poster with a short explanation about how and where to weed, cultivate soil, and harvest flowers and vegetables. Watering with the hose should be supervised or done by experienced staff only.

❑ Contact a local mission, homeless shelter, or food pantry about future donations of extra garden produce.

Potpourri

Texture: Flowers and leaves

Herb: Lavender

Houseplant: Spider plant (*Chlorophytum comosum*)

Tree: Lemon (*Citrus lemon* "Ponderosa"). Can be grown indoors.

Flower: Nasturtium (*Tropaeolum majus*). This annual's variegated leaves are especially attractive. Flowers and leaves, when grown using *only* organic methods, look and taste great in salads (peppery flavor).

Wildlife: Rabbits

Garden Club Meeting Ideas

• Make stepping stones from quick drying cement with sturdy cardboard box forms placed on boards for support. Create "in-laid" designs from various objects pressed into the cement. Provide gloves for hand protection.

• **Speaker:** Learn about the honeybee. Contact a local Master Gardener or beekeeper.

• Discuss old-time herbal remedies. Serve commercially prepared herbal tea.

• Discuss gourds and their uses. Is there room in the garden for them?

• Plant seeds and plants of warm weather crops in raised beds and container gardens (e.g., cucumbers, squash, tomatoes, pole beans, annual herbs and flowers).

• **Book of the Month:** Kress, S. W. (Ed.). (1998). *Bird gardens*. Pownal, VT: Storey Books.

Spontaneous Interactions

• Take individual residents for a walk in the garden whenever possible.

• Look for insects. Capture them (if there is a good supply). Discuss them with residents.

• Have a lightweight, solid plastic container available to hold mulch or compost. Place mulch in the container, and ask a resident in a wheelchair to carry it. Place a towel over the resident's lap, and distribute the mulch in the garden together.

• Cut a single large bloom and give it to a family member.

Having Fun with Kids

• Show how roots grow. Cut off the narrow neck of a plastic milk container; then cut out two "TV screen" windows on opposite sides of the container. Cover the windows from the inside with heavy clear plastic (e.g., overhead acetate). Fill the container with soil, and plant bean seeds close to the windows.

Cover windows with dark cloth or construction paper, and remove covering to observe.

- Begin a scarecrow project. Decide what materials are needed, which ones the children will provide, and which supplies the Home will contribute.

- Start an insect log. Walk around the garden asking children to point out bugs. List the names or make simple sketches for later identification.

- **Book:** Ryder, J. (1999). *Snail's spell*. New York, NY: Frederick Warne.

June

Now is the time to be sure that the Garden Team is in place. Watering and weed control are essential from now on, with special attention paid to the smaller containers that dry out and need frequent watering. Residents can be part of the "bug patrol" to track down insects before they take over a crop. Prevention is the key: water early, spray off aphids and spider mites, keep full-sun beds mulched, and handpick tomato worms and Japanese beetles.

Indoor Plant Care

Daily

- ❏ Routine observation of indoor plants.
- ❏ Are leaves on outdoor trees or shrubs shading sun-loving plants?

Weekly

- ❏ Routine indoor plant care; resident personal plant care.
- ❏ Observe pruned plants for new growth.
- ❏ Observe for drying out of indoor pots and containers. How is the increased sun and air conditioning affecting the indoor plants? Are the large floor plants mulched to reduce evaporation from the soil?

Monthly

- ❏ Post indoor and outdoor schedules. Hold Plant Team meetings when possible. Place events on the calendar.
- ❏ Share indoor plant changes with other Neighborhoods.
- ❏ Take pictures!
- ❏ Consider using time-release fertilizer pellets in houseplants to reduce need to fertilize.

Outdoor Garden Care

Daily

- ❏ Spot weeding and deadheading of outdoor plants.
- ❏ Observe new crops for insects; treat ASAP.

- ❏ Use *Bacillus thurengiensis* (i.e., Dipel) on soft-bodied caterpillars on tomatoes; follow instruction on can.
- ❏ Check toad abode's water dish.
- ❏ Fill birdbath.

Weekly

- ❏ Consider dividing garden tasks into sections of the garden to be done on certain days. For example, raised beds on Monday and Tuesday; vegetables in ground beds on Wednesday; trellis on Thursday, and so forth. Share this idea with Garden Team(s).
- ❏ Observe for drying out of outdoor containers, raised beds, and ground beds. Are the outdoor containers drying within a few days, or can they still be watered only once a week?
- ❏ Are the outdoor gardens mulched to reduce the need to water?
- ❏ Harvest crops as needed. Some greens will be going to seed (i.e., bolting) and the leaves will taste bitter. Pull these and add to the compost

pile. Plant bush beans or other warm-weather crops in their place.

Monthly

❑ Post Garden Team schedules. Hold Garden Team meetings when possible. Place events on the calendar.

❑ Share garden happenings with the Neighborhood Teams.

❑ Try *succession planting* of seeds to keep a steady supply of crops such as bush beans and heat-tolerant lettuce. Use bush and dwarf types whenever possible. Pull up the fading plants, renew the compost or fertilizer, and plant seeds or young plants.

❑ Hold an informal garden party for the volunteers and Plant Teams.

❑ Prune lower branches and leaves of upright vegetables such as tomatoes, eggplants, and peppers to provide good air circulation and reduce insect damage.

❑ Take pictures!

Potpourri

Texture: Cotton fibers

Herb: Mint (*Mentha*; all kinds)

Houseplant: Begonia (e.g., Angel wing, Rex, Reiger)

Flower: Snapdragon (*Antirrhinum majus*). Annual in the north; may winter over in warmer locations.

Tree: Ginko (*Ginko biloba;* zones 5–10)

Wildlife: Lacewing (*Chrysopa rufilabris*). Lacewing is a beneficial insect.

Garden Club Meeting Ideas

• Cut and arrange flowers and foliage from the garden for dining room tables, the reception desk, laundry personnel, and so forth.

• Make a salad from the garden produce.

• Discuss how to control slugs, white flies, and Colorado potato beetles.

• Make or buy a bug catching net and use it.

• Mix up some **homebrew bug spray** using 4–5 cloves of fresh garlic, ¼ cup hot pepper sauce, a few drops of vegetable oil, and 3–5 drops of pure soap (e.g., Ivory). Mix in a blender with a cup of hot water. Pour into a container with lid, and let sit for a day. Strain through cheesecloth. Add to a gallon of water. Apply to tops and bottoms of infested leaves with a spray bottle.

• **Books of the Month:** Riotte, L. (1987). *Sleeping with a sunflower: A treasury of old-time garden lore.* Pownal, VT: Storey Books. James, T. (1990). *The potpourri gardener.* New York, NY: Hungry Minds.

Spontaneous Interactions

• Take a resident to pick flowers for potpourri.

• Watch for hummingbirds on the cardinal climber vine.

• Ask a resident to help tie up a tomato vine or stake a perennial.

• Offer herbal tea to residents with visitors.

• Do mini rounds of the houseplants with a resident. Look for wilting, insects, candy wrappers, and gum in the pots.

Having Fun with Kids

• Take slides of current garden activities.

• Finish the scarecrow.

• Use child-sized garden tools and watering cans. Teach kids to use them correctly.

• As plants go to seed, collect seeds in plastic bags; label with name of plant and color.

• Look at flowers and insects through a magnifying glass.

• Press flowers in old telephone books. Dry flowers in cornmeal and borax following instructions found in the University of Missouri pamphlet *Drying Flowers and Foliage for Arrangements* (Rothenberger, 2000).

• **Book:** Loewer, P. and Loewer, J. (1997). *The moonflower.* Atlanta, GA: Peachtree Press.

July

As vegetables mature, consistent watering is vital to prevent blossom end rot, and produce evenly formed crops. Be aware of effects of air conditioning and strong sunshine on indoor plants. The green spaces indoors will be a welcome haven for residents and visitors. Begin to plan for fall crops like turnips, broccoli, or salad greens, and fall flowers to brighten front entrances and outdoor seating areas.

Indoor Plant Care

Daily

❑ Be sure houseplants placed outdoors are grouped according to light needs. Plants placed close together can be watered at the same time with a soft spray from the hose and will create a mutually moist atmosphere.

❑ Deadhead flowering houseplants.

Weekly

❑ Watering is especially important. Check soil in containers by poking finger at least an inch below the surface. Use water meters on large pots.

❑ Routine indoor plant care and resident personal plant care.

❑ Restock plant cart.

Monthly

❑ Post schedule for Plant Teams.

❑ Stay consistent with plant care. Call in extra volunteers to cover vacations.

❑ Don't forget to fertilize houseplants.

Outdoor Garden Care

Daily

❑ During walks around the garden, spot-check for insects.

❑ Garden spiders can be interesting. Consider capturing one in a jar temporarily to show to residents and children. (Handle with care—they can bite!)

❑ Deadhead flowers; harvest crops as needed.

Weekly

❑ Watering is especially important. Check soil in containers by poking finger at least an inch below the surface. Use a water meter with large containers.

❑ Cucumbers, tomatoes, and squash need thorough and consistent watering as they mature. Read up on blossom end rot of tomatoes.

❑ Harvest zucchini and summer squash when no more than 5–6 inches long and the skin is still thin enough to be marked by a fingernail. These can be used raw in salads, or make stir-fry dishes with them for lunch.

❑ Check fertilizing schedule. Use time-release fertilizer when possible; side-dress with compost if available.

❑ Replace mulch as needed to keep in valuable moisture and reduce weeds.

❑ Cut flowers to dry (see Rothenberger, 2002)

❑ Look for new starts of cool weather flowers (e.g., flowering kale, mums) and vegetables (e.g., broccoli, Brussels sprouts) in garden centers. Plant for color and fall harvest; start seeds of turnips directly in garden bed for late harvest.

Monthly

❑ Post schedule for Garden Teams.

❑ Hold a garden produce tea party.

❑ Fill in spots in flower gardens where earlier annuals have died back. Use seedlings coming up elsewhere, leftover lettuce or salad greens seeds, extra plants still in small pots, or donations from garden centers in these areas.

Potpourri

Texture: Stones

Herb: Sweet basil (*Ocimum basilicum*)

Houseplant: Polka-dot plant (*Hypoestes phyllostachya*)

Flower: Roses (many varieties). Select according to hardiness in your zone.

Tree: Pecan (*Carya illinoiensis*; zones 6–9)

Wildlife: Hummingbirds

Garden Club Meeting Ideas

• Pick red, white, and blue flowers for tables.

• Evaluate the Home's garden for advice about changes or improvements, and ideas for next year.

• Discuss entering the County Fair. Are there any unusual or especially nice flowers or vegetables worthy of display? Contact the local Fair Board for entry information.

• Discuss Calendula (*Calendula officinalis*; also known as pot marigold). Use fresh in salads.

• Ask an expert floral arranger from a local florist or garden club to demonstrate the use of flowers and foliage from the Home's gardens.

• **Book of the Month:** Bailey, L. (1985). *Country flowers: Gardening bouquets from spring to fall*. New York, NY: Random House.

Spontaneous Interactions

• Catch a ladybug, Japanese beetle, daddy-longlegs, lightning bug, or other slow moving "bug" and show it off.

• Point out two hummingbird-attracting flowers. Find a picture of a hummingbird.

• Pick a dozen different kinds of leaves from outside plants and examine them.

• Use scissors to deadhead the African violets and angel wing begonias.

• Pick three fragrant flowers or leaves and compare them.

Having Fun with Kids

• Sift compost using a handmade or purchased sifter. Collect sifted compost in a container and spread on vegetable bed.

• Show kids around the garden. Point out items already collected to make small bouquets to hang and dry at home. Cut, make into bunches, wrap with rubber band and narrow ribbon. Include flowers, herbs, interesting twigs, grasses, and leaves.

• Work in the kids' garden together.

• Take herb cuttings. Pot up cuttings in margarine tubs with holes punched for drainage and use the lids for saucers. Use rooting hormone as needed. Place in a protected, but bright spot in garden.

• **Book:** Crebbin, J. (1995). *Danny's duck*. Cambridge, MA: Candlewick Press.

August

Harvesting is in full swing by now with salads and vegetables available for snacks, or for sending home with the children. Flowers and fragrant herbs can be cut and made into wreaths for fall fund-raising, or completed and stored for a Christmas bazaar. Cuttings can be taken from houseplants that might have grown too large to be brought back inside. Would residents enjoy entering flowers and vegetables in the local County Fair? Call the County Extension Agent for Fair entrance details.

Indoor Plant Care

Daily

- ❑ Watch plants for wilting caused by too much air conditioning or direct sun.

Weekly

- ❑ Maintain residents' personal plants and public area plants.
- ❑ With residents' input, bring in or order a new flowering plant from a catalog for a general lift in spirits.

Monthly

- ❑ Fertilize houseplants.
- ❑ Cultivate around plants as needed, and add mulch.

Outdoor Garden Care

Daily

- ❑ Water as early in the morning as possible.
- ❑ Make sure houseplants placed outside are not in the scorching sun.

Weekly

- ❑ Continue weeding, pest control, deadheading, and harvesting.
- ❑ Keep an eye on new fall crop transplants and seedlings. Water and thin as needed.
- ❑ Take extra produce to the city mission, food bank, or sell to staff and visitors.

- ❑ This is the last month to feed roses and other established perennials.
- ❑ Cut back bloomed-out perennials, but retain foliage.
- ❑ Keep seed pods picked off begonias and continue to deadhead.
- ❑ Cut back and fertilize annuals for renewed cool-weather blooming.

Monthly

- ❑ Look for sprouting acorns of white oaks. Save them to plant with children.
- ❑ Thin turnips and other fall seedlings.
- ❑ Cut and hang flowers and foliage to dry.
- ❑ Look for sources of wild grapevine. Ask volunteers to gather it for wreaths.
- ❑ Cultivate around plants as needed, and replace mulch.
- ❑ Turn the compost pile and keep it moist. Add untreated grass clippings; mix well.

Potpourri

Texture: Nuts (e.g., acorns, peanuts, walnuts, hazelnuts, buckeyes). Use caution with inedible nuts.

Herb: Scented geranium (*Pelargonium*). Varieties include lemon, rose, nutmeg, and lime.

Houseplant: Moses in the cradle (*Rhoeo spathacea*)

Flower: Butterfly weed (*Asclepias; A. incarnata* and *A. tuberosa*). A perennial butterfly-attracting plant, hardy in zones 3–9. Seeds can be planted directly into the garden bed in the fall—easy!

Tree: Sea grape (*Coccoloba uvifera*; zones 9b and 10)

Wildlife: Bats

Garden Club Meeting Ideas

- Make **rosemary lemonade**: Mix well in a saucepan 1 heaping teaspoon dried rosemary or 2 teaspoons fresh, and 1 cup water; boil gently for five minutes. Strain rosemary. Add enough liquid to make 3 cups of seasoned water. Add 1 small can frozen lemonade (thawed), and a pinch of salt. Serve over ice. To use a large frozen lemonade, adjust herb to taste. Ginger ale may be substituted for a portion of the water (from The Gathering Basket Herb Society, Hancock County, OH).

- Preserve hydrangea blossoms, fall-colored oak and maple leaves, and eucalyptus branches in glycerin. Use one third glycerin to two thirds hot water. Pound the ends of stems to flatten, and place in 4 inches of solution until the majority of fluid is absorbed. See *Flowercrafts* (Wood and Merer, 1985). Pharmacies carry glycerin.

- Discuss getting produce ready for the County Fair.

- Borrow or have a greenhouse representative bring exotic blooming flowers to discuss.

- Start pots of various kinds of wheat grass. Take cuttings of catmint for feline residents.

- Invite the local garden club to a meeting.

- **Book of the Month:** Wood, E. and Merer, J. (1985). *Flowercrafts: Decorating and designing with flowers and floral motifs.* New York, NY: HarperCollins.

Spontaneous Interactions

- Drag out the wading pool, and have a foot splashing party.

- Pick a small bouquet with a resident. Arrange them in corsage style in a holder; pin it on the resident.

- Make a hollyhock doll.

- "Take five" (or ten) in the shade with a sprig of fresh lavender (inhale deeply), and enjoy a glass of iced tea with fresh mint leaves.

Having Fun with Kids

- Make ice cubes with edible flowers. *Use only organically raised flowers.* Rinse flower heads well; and freeze in the ice cube tray. Use in drinks the next day. Try lavender, calendula, pansies, rose petals, herb flowers, alyssum, cornflower, cosmos, daisy, or honeysuckle.

- Hold an indoor "fill the flower pot" race. Form two teams for a relay race. Each child fills a plastic pot with garden soil, walks fast across the room to a bucket, dumps the soil, walks back to the next child, and hands him or her the pot and trowel, and so on.

- Make bookmarks using pressed, dried flowers and wax paper. Iron the pressed flowers between sheets of precut wax paper. Glue to slightly larger colored construction paper backing; punch a hole in the top edge. Loop and tie yarn through the hole.

- Show slides of current intergenerational activities.

- **Book:** Charner, K. (Ed.) (1997). *Everything for fall—A complete activity book for teachers of young children: Activities for September, October and November.* Beltsville, MD: Gryphon House.

September

Time for houseplants that have been vacationing out on the patio to move back inside. Green spaces fill up again with plants lush from summer growth. A new spurt of growing energy comes from taking cuttings and starting seeds. Some residents will welcome their "babies" back home; others will be tired of them. Time to renew or update community garden club contacts.

The outdoor garden is too pretty to pull up, but is coming to a close. Instead of mourning the end of the season, think of all that great compost material provided by the annuals. In warmer climates, another phase of growing is about to begin!

Indoor Plant Care

Daily

❏ In northern climates, prepare to bring houseplants back inside before nighttime temperatures dip below 65°F. Is their former spot still available? Have some plants grown too large for their location? Is there a saucer for each pot?

❏ Spray each plant thoroughly with a commercial brand, Ivory, or Fels Naptha soap solution, and rinse off by the end of the day before moving inside. Check the leaves, soil surface, and bottom of the pot for insects and other freeloading critters. Wipe the summer's dust off the pot and saucer.

❏ Some plants will experience stress due to the change from outside to inside temperature and light conditions. Shorter autumn days also play a part in leaf loss and a slowing of growth. Ficus trees often drop leaves if moved too quickly. They will lose a minimal amount of leaves if brought in while the outside temperature is comparable to the facility's inside temperature.

To reduce relocation shock: Prune the ficus tree, relocate it for at least a week to a spot with less light outside (two weeks is preferable; this is termed *acclimatization*), and then take it inside to its permanent location.

To prune a ficus: Use clean, sharp scissors or pruners to remove uneven growth and long, scraggly branches. Make the cut on woody growth just outside the *branch bark collar* (a rough, circular line of bark at the base of the branch). Thin out overlapping branches. Generally shape the tree to the desired height and width while trying to maintain a natural appearance.

Weekly

❏ Routine plant maintenance.

❏ Prune and acclimatize houseplants that spent the summer outside; check for insects and treat with soap spray.

❏ Routine resident personal plant care.

❏ Residents might have lost interest in their plants; discuss choices for a different kind of plant.

❏ Clean the light shelves and light tubes with disinfectant.

❏ Place rooted herb cuttings in the sunniest exposures or on the light shelves.

❏ If using a liquid fertilizer, this will be the last month to fertilize until early spring. If using time-released pellets, check to see when they need renewing.

Monthly

❏ Have light shelves in operation by the end of the month.

❏ Start a few houseplant seed varieties on light shelves.

❏ Order a few exotic and vining flowering plants from catalogs or get donations for appropriate windows or light shelves. Be sure to order before the cold weather sets in.

❏ Replace mulch in larger pots as needed.

❏ Examine each indoor plant for insect invasion; treat with soap spray or alcohol swabs as needed.

❏ Purchase a supply of potting mix or mix up ingredients. Have commercial or homemade soap spray on hand. Replace worn out sponges; renew rag supply.

❏ Stay in touch with local garden clubs for mentoring and donations.

Outdoor Plant Care

Daily

❏ Pick and enjoy flowers and vegetables while they last.

❏ Watch for migrating birds.

❏ Continue to water as needed.

❏ Watch for seed pod formation, but **do not remove.**

❏ Observe which birds eat which seeds.

Weekly

❏ Routine plant care.

❏ Keep mulch in place and weeds pulled in the fall vegetable garden.

❏ Observe which trees turn color and drop leaves first.

❏ Ask to have mower-mulched leaves from the Home's grounds added to the compost pile.

❏ Discuss planting spring bulbs in beds outside, and in pots inside for forcing.

❏ Gather and hang or preserve flowers, herbs, and foliage for drying.

Monthly

❏ Post Garden Team schedule and discuss tasks to be done with staff and volunteers.

❏ **Begin garden cleanup.** Try to do this each week from now on to reduce workload (e.g., pull spent tomato plants but save a few tomatoes to ripen on windowsills; pull annuals *without* seeds of interest to birds; remove and salvage any reusable plant markers; remove, clean, and store plant stakes and cages; leave annual vines in place for bird hiding places, but remove them before nesting time next year; pick up sticks and branches to add to the brush pile for animal cover).

❏ Discuss installing a heated water dish for birds or adding a heating device to the birdbath for a winter supply of water.

❏ Send out a newsletter update about garden and nature happenings with a Human Habitat "wish list" for holiday giving.

Potpourri

Texture: Moss (several kinds)

Herb: Thyme (*Thymus*; any variety)

Houseplant: Jasmine (*Tracheolospermum jasminoides*). Research the type most appropriate for your indoor location. Many produce fragrant blooms. Some are winter bloomers which need cool temperatures. Most are vining.

Flower: *Chrysanthemum* (mum). Hardy in zones 4–8; look for a type that doesn't need pinching back.

Tree: Beauty berry (*Callicarpa americana;* zones 7–10)

Wildlife: Deer

Garden Club Meeting Ideas

- Discuss choice of houseplant seeds and exotic plants. Order, and plant or pot up.

- Is anyone willing to try to bring last year's poinsettia back into bloom? It's quite a commitment, but fun. Contrary to long-standing belief, poinsettias are not toxic to the average person or animal. Check with the Extension Office or agricultural department of a local university. To induce your plant to bloom, keep it in a sunny window until October 1. Then, place it in a lighttight box (absolutely no cracks or holes) at 5:00 p.m. and remove it 8:00 a.m. daily. This must be done consistently for results. Continue to water and fertilize with a full-strength flower fertilizer according to directions. Color should begin to show in the top leaves by the third week in November. When color appears, stop using the box, and enjoy the show.

- Do the residents want any new perennials planted? Can starts be obtained from families or neighbors?

- Start thinking about making holiday decorations using natural materials (as fire codes will allow). An outdoor wreath for the birds might be interesting. Start now by finding grapevine, choosing a site, making, and hanging a wreath. When the natural food supply in the garden dwindles, start adding goodies to the wreath (around mid-to-late November).

- **Book of the Month:** National Wildlife Federation. (1974). *Gardening with wildlife*. Washington, DC: Author.

Spontaneous Interactions

- Unwrap part of a frost-killed vine and make a mini-wreath. Add some herbs and flower heads for decoration.

- Watch a sunrise or sunset with a resident.

- Look up an unusual bird seen in the yard.

- Gather a bag full of autumn leaves with a resident. Check them for bugs, then scatter them on the dining room tables.

Having Fun with Kids

- Construct a "feel box" by cutting a hand-sized hole in a box for adults and children to insert one hand. Fasten a piece of cloth to drape over the hole to prevent the contents from being seen. Collect an assortment of natural objects for them to identify (e.g., feathers, nuts, dried bean pods, stones, animal bones, sturdy leaves, a flower seed head, lichen, cotton balls).

- Work with kids and residents to clean up the kids' garden.

- Plant some hardy annual or perennial seeds in the children's garden. Mark the spot. Talk about the seeds "sleeping" through the winter, and "waking up" in the spring.

- Harvest the sunflower heads; decide what to do with the seeds.

- **Book:** Herr, J., Larson, Y., and Libbey, Y. (1997). *Creative resources: Birds and animals*. Albany, NY: Delmar Learning.

October

The days are much shorter, so plants are getting less natural light. The furnace is starting to run, and the tagalong outdoor insects are looking for juicy, comfortable homes in the nooks and crannies of houseplants. Herb cuttings are slowing down, but still smell great. The blooming African violets and begonias on the light shelves keep the spirit of new life in full view of residents and staff.

The outdoor garden is ready for cleaning, turning over, and the application of mulched leaves, grass, or shredded garden debris. Cool weather crops are harvested. Warmer climates will continue to nourish and enjoy hardy annuals and vegetables.

This is a wonderful time for cutting and drying herbs and everlastings for autumn display and winter bouquets.

Indoor Plant Care

Daily

❏ Be alert to locations of heating ducts in relation to plants. Warm air circulation is good, but can lead to rapid drying of leaves and soil. This can result in wilting and spider mite infestation. Direct sunlight on shade-loving or bright light-loving plants can produce similar problems. Take advantage of the good effects of the heat by placing the pots in trays or containers of pebbles, and adding water to the trays below the level of the bottom of the pot.

❏ Group plants to increase the overall humidity; spot-check for mites and mealy bugs.

❏ Don't forget poinsettia care.

❏ A maximum–minimum thermometer will keep track of the low and high temperatures in the sunroom or other green spaces. Residents will enjoy checking it each day.

Weekly

❏ Resident personal plant care. Residents may be interested in adopting some houseplant seedlings from the light shelves.

❏ Cats might be eager to chew on new foliage; offer them pots of grass and catnip instead.

❏ If low humidity is a problem, try setting small buckets of water among the plants. Keep the buckets out of the way of people traffic. Don't worry if the dogs drink out of them.

❏ If drafty windows are a problem, consider taping clear plastic sheeting over them. Check for blasts of cold air on plants from open doorways.

Monthly

❏ Post Plant and Garden Team(s) schedules.

❏ Hold joint Neighborhood and Plant Team meeting to review winter care and problem prevention measures.

❏ Write an article for the facility newsletter.

❏ Renew contacts with local newspapers for "green and growing" interviews.

❏ Check for leaking pots or saucers and replace.

❏ Are the residents' green spaces comfortable for people as well as plants? If some plants have outgrown their locations, cut back the longer growth or consider donating them to local child day centers or schools.

❏ Consider ways to increase light in low-light plant spaces. Consider mirrors, white paint, light shelves, and so forth.

Outdoor Garden Care

Daily

❏ As time allows, cut herbs, flowers, and foliage for drying and preserving.

❏ Clip stalks with seed heads and bunch together to hang for bird snacks.

❏ Watch the temperature forecast. If tomatoes are still ripening, frost-protection may be needed.

Weekly

❏ When frost kills foliage on tuberous begonias, gladiolas, and dahlias, gently dig around the plants and lift out the tubers. Shake off the dirt, and place the tubers in an above freezing storage area to dry. Pack them in sand or sawdust to prevent shriveling.

❏ Continue to clean up garden debris.

❏ Discard old roots, stems, and foliage of annual plants.

❏ Spread mower-chopped leaves and grass clippings, or baled straw over garden beds.

❏ If this is the first year to mulch, consider spading up the vegetable bed. With consistent mulching, this back-bending chore **won't** need repeating.

Monthly

❏ Plant Team and volunteer schedule, post garden calendar.

❏ Start placing ears of corn on the squirrel feeders.

❏ Keep the birdbath full and clean.

❏ Before storing tools, clean and oil metal parts, and wax or treat wooden handles.

Potpourri

Texture: Wool (many forms). Find fleece from sheep, yarn, cloth, socks, and other forms.

Herb: Sorrel, broad-leafed French (*Rumex scutatus*)

Houseplant: Night-blooming Cereus (*Epiphyllum oxypetalum*; also known as Dutchman's pipe)

Flower: Hardy Bear's breeches (*Acanthus balcanicus,* perennial in zones 6–10)

Tree: Eastern red cedar (*Juniperus virginiana*; zones 2–8)

Wildlife: Duck (talk about most common local type)

Garden Club Meeting Ideas

• Redecorate the birds' wreath with peanut butter and birdseed pinecones, bags of suet, and staghorn sumac berry clusters.

• Read the *Farmer's Almanac* chapter for the month.

• Collect and examine all seed pods in the garden and from trees and shrubs. If a field is near the facility, collect all available seeds. Discard unidentifiable seeds from the field to prevent weed invasion. Discuss wild birds and their seed preferences.

• Discuss purchasing and planting spring bulbs outdoors. Can adequate precautions be taken to prevent children, confused residents, and animals from eating toxic bulbs? Be sure the Neighborhood Team is aware of this issue and your decision.

• **Book of the Month:** Simmons, A. G. (1992). *Herb gardening in five seasons: An illustrated guide to cultivating herbs for recipes, decorations and gifts*. New York, NY: E. P. Dutton.

Spontaneous Interactions

- Take a willing resident outside to cut flowers for drying; bunch and hang them with the resident's name on a tag.

- Snip available catmint; hang it to dry for cat toys.

- Fill the bird feeder or birdbath. Look for birds eating the flower seed heads.

- Look up the resident's personal plant in a plant book.

Having Fun with Kids

- Make pumpkin and spice ice cream. At the beginning of the session, mix pumpkin pie spices with canned pumpkin and swirl it through softened vanilla ice cream in small containers. Place the mixture in the freezer until the end of session.

- Plant spring bulbs outside. Take precautions against people or animals ingesting the bulbs.

- Make birdseed pictures with white glue on construction paper (e.g., kids' and residents' initials). Talk about different kinds of birdseed.

- Examine the bird feeders together. Are they in good shape or do they need repairs?

- **Book:** Sanders, S. R. (1998). *Warm as wool*. New York, NY: Aladdin Paperbacks.

November

Most indoor plants are now back inside and have settled into the slower way of life with lower light and shorter days. Cuttings have rooted, house-plant seeds are sprouting, and holiday gift plants are arriving.

The outdoor gardens are almost tucked in for the winter, with a few hardy annuals left for color in moderate zones. A new round of growing begins in year-round gardening areas.

Limit the number of new plants started as the holiday season approaches, but be sure to try a few exotic and unusual plants to rejuvenate resident and staff interest.

Indoor Plant Care

Daily

- ❏ Check for water in pebble trays; add more if needed. Hot air heat will be drying out the atmosphere.
- ❏ Ask (or leave a note for) night staff to check if the lights on the shelves are coming on at the expected time.
- ❏ Spot-check for mulch and remove trash from plant containers.

Weekly

- ❏ Routine plant care. Continue with record-keeping as appropriate.
- ❏ Resident plant care.
- ❏ Transplant rooted cuttings as needed.
- ❏ Consider a mini in-service for resident and community volunteers to renew the growing spirit, and update on the greenery.
- ❏ Start reducing water for certain plants (e.g., cacti, certain succulents; see individual requirements). Check plant care log about starting to increase watering for others such as amaryllis. **Insert instruction labels with plants as needed**.

Monthly

- ❏ Post Plant Team and volunteer schedules; post garden calendar.

- ❏ Fertilize light cart plants only according to the schedule.
- ❏ Enjoy the results of the poinsettia care.
- ❏ Spot-check plants' shape to see if they are being rotated a quarter turn each week.

Outdoor Garden Care

Daily

- ❏ Enjoy those last warm days of autumn by turning the compost, spreading more leaves and straw on the beds, and cutting back scraggly perennials.
- ❏ Pull the last of the tomato vines, clip off the root ball, and hang in a frost-free location while the remaining tomatoes ripen. If this isn't practical, pick remaining green tomatoes, wrap them in newspaper, and place in cool location to ripen.

Weekly

- ❏ If this is the first year to mulch the vegetable garden, consider spading the beds prior to mulching. With consistent mulching, this chore won't need to be repeated.

❏ Pick all remaining decorative flowers and foliage, add branches of autumn leaves. Place the arrangement where residents and visitors can enjoy it.

❏ Check nighttime temperatures. Ask residents about frost and freeze warnings.

❏ If rain has been scarce, water perennials and shrubs thoroughly before freezing weather sets in.

❏ Consider a small, live Christmas tree for outside decoration. If appropriate, ask a local garden club to donate the tree and plant it. Choose a well-drained spot near a window which allows for adequate growing space. Ask about the rate of growth and eventual size of the tree. Ask your Master Gardener to assist with the planting if needed.

Monthly

❏ Post Plant Team schedules, and gardening calendar.

❏ Write an article for the newsletter.

❏ Turn the compost pile once more before it freezes; keep adding those banana peels.

❏ Be sure the paths are swept clean.

❏ Clean and oil tools and equipment then put away for the winter.

❏ Is a heating coil for the birdbath in place?

❏ Are there any more bulbs to be planted?

Potpourri

Texture: Snake skin (from a live snake and a discarded skin).

Herb: Sage (*Salvia officinalis*; perennial in zones 5–8)

Houseplant: Bamboo palm (*Chamaedorea erumpens*)

Flower: Orchids. Find a reliable source, and ask for an easy to grow variety.

Tree: Royal poinciana (*Delonix regia,* zone 10)

Wildlife: Garden snake (local varieties)

Garden Club Meeting Ideas

• Invite local gourd expert to demonstrate gourd use.

• Dry sage from the garden to use in turkey dressing.

• Discuss a "wish list" for garden tools and equipment, books and magazines, and items for gardening activities. Post this in the newsletter and include it in a holiday greeting to the garden clubs.

• Invite local orchid grower to discuss how to grow this plant.

• Start topiaries from rooted herb cuttings.

• **Book of the Month:** Felton, E. (1992). *Artistically cultivated herbs*. Santa Barbara, CA: Woodbridge Press.

Spontaneous Interactions

• Talk about the shape of trees after the leaves have dropped; look at different types.

• Examine new seedlings or the poinsettia.

• Pull some late parsley and nibble on a piece with a resident. Check diet and allergies first.

• Check the late autumn crops for growth.

• Mix a small batch of potting soil.

Having Fun With Kids

• Ask a local pet shop or zoo to bring in a small, nonaggressive snake and other reptiles.

• *Snake homes.* Have a selection of rocks, sticks, leaves, soil, and so forth in shoe boxes for kids and residents to construct their own versions of snake houses.

• *"Who lives in this house?" game.* Show pictures or have actual "houses" of various animals and insects (e.g., birdhouse, cocoon, log with hollow section, bird nest, pile of small rocks, chrysalis, a cave, bee hive, spider web, hornet's nest).

• **Book:** McNulty, F. (1994). *A snake in the house*. New York, NY: Scholastic.

December

The holiday season will be uppermost in the daily routines of most Homes. As the outdoor gardens rest or take a backseat to inside preparations, flowering indoor gift plants will appear, and will need appropriate space.

Herbs can be used in delightful aromatic and culinary ways to symbolize ethnic and seasonal celebrations.

Indoor Plant Care

Daily

- Watch for the appearance of gift plants which might be harmful to residents or animals (e.g., ornamental peppers, holly with berries, any kind of berries or unidentified fruit). Ask for the source of the plant if it can't be identified and/or call a plant mentor for information.
- Spot-check for yellowing or dead leaves and twigs, and remove.

Weekly

- Routine resident plant care. May need to relocate plants as gift plants arrive. Add gift plants to the care list.
- Routine Neighborhood plant care. Try to give the green spaces a good cleanup to encourage relatives and visitors to enjoy their time with residents.
- Be alert to effects of heat and changing sunlight exposure on plants. Watch for spider mites and mealy bugs.
- Are water-rooted cuttings or seedlings overdue for transplanting?
- Take herb cuttings for decorations or for residents who want to include a sprig in holiday cards (e.g., "rosemary for remembrance," thyme, pressed lamb's ear leaves).

Monthly

- Stay in touch with volunteers. Is there a plan for a holiday event or recognition for them?

- Check on bulbs being forced. Is there any growth yet?
- Take time to enjoy the beauty of the green spaces. Sit for five minutes and observe the texture, color, and fragrance of the variety of plants.
- Routine indoor Plant Care schedule.
- Calendar notes or event.

Outdoor Garden Care

Daily

- In warmer climates where outdoor production continues, check for watering and fertilizing needs. Continue to pick and harvest.
- If a warm spell develops, bundle up a resident and go outside with a broom to sweep the paths.
- Check the birdbath and feeders. Orange peels and apple cores can be shared with the wildlife. Don't keep the peels inside for more than a couple days.

Weekly

- Make sure the heating coil in the birdbath is working.

- Add goodies to the birds' wreath (e.g., suet, flower seed heads, orange slices).

- Mulch the ground around perennials after the ground freezes. Pile leaves around roses and enclose them with a wire cage.

- Begin looking ahead to the New Year with garden catalogs.

- Think about additions to and changes for next year's garden.

- Begin to list choices for plants, crops, and improvements for next year.

Potpourri

Texture: Individual types of bird seed (e.g., safflower, milo, sunflower, thistle, mixed, millet, cracked corn)

Herb: Rosemary (*Rosmarinus officinalis*). See *Growing and Using Rosemary* (Reppert, 1996).

Houseplant: African violet (*Saintpaulia* hybrids)

Flower: Passion flower (*Passiflora* varieties). A vining plant with spectacular flowers. Logee's in Connecticut carries them; call toll-free: 1–888–330–8038.

Tree: Silver dollar gum (*Eucalyptus polyanthemos*; zones 6b–10)

Wildlife: Opossum

Garden Club Meeting Ideas

- Design and create a natural wreath for the outside front door. Use all dried garden materials and items from the wild (e.g., preserved flowers and foliage, meadow and woods weeds, fungi, lichen-covered twigs and branches, feathers, large leaves, moss).

- Make food using rosemary as the seasoning. Supply the kitchen with rosemary for selected recipes.

- Study the passion plant—its origin, many varieties, and cultivation. Do the same with the eucalyptus tree.

- Ask a Division of Wildlife representative to talk about the "possum."

- **Book of the Month:** Cox, F. (1995). *Seasons in a country garden.* Golden, CO: Fulcrum Publishing.

Spontaneous Interactions

- Point out frozen ponds or water as soon as it occurs.

- Look through a new seed catalog with a resident.

- Take the bird food bucket with apple cores and bread scraps outside along with a willing resident. Ask the resident to throw the scraps to the birds.

- Pick off (if plentiful) an indoor flower and examine closely with a resident. Use a magnifying glass and plenty of light.

Having Fun with Kids

- What do animals do in the winter? How do they eat, sleep, and stay warm?

- Make and serve rosemary lemonade.

- *"Birds in our yard reports."* Divide resident–child teams into groups with names of garden birds. Hand out sheets of paper with clearly printed information about each type of bird (e.g., name, feather colors, food preferences), and a picture of each bird. Bring groups back together and have a resident–child team describe each bird.

- Talk about the eucalyptus tree and its favorite animal, the koala. Bring in stuffed koala bear toys.

- **Book:** Sharp, A. (1995). *The koala book.* Gretna, LA: Pelican Publishing.

- **Book:** Herriot, J. (1986). *The Christmas day kitten.* New York, NY: St. Martin's Press.

References and Resources

Gardening for People with Special Needs

Adil, J. R. (1994). *Accessible gardening for people with physical disabilities: A guide to methods, tools, and plants*. Bethesda, MD: Woodbine House.

American Horticultural Therapy Association. (1995). *Plant projects for patients with Alzheimer's disease*. Gaithersburg, MD: Author.

De Hart, M. R. and Brown, J. R. (2001). *Horticultural therapy: A guide for all seasons*. St. Louis, MO: National Garden Clubs, Inc. *Available from:* National Garden Clubs, Inc. Member Services, 4401 Magnolia Avenue, St. Louis, MO 63110.

Garden Center of Greater Cleveland. (n.d.). *Therapeutic gardening*. Cleveland, OH: Author. Available from: The Garden Center of Greater Cleveland, 11030 East Boulevard, Cleveland, OH 44106. *Phone:* 216–721–1600.

Rothert, G. (1994). *The enabling garden: A guide to lifelong gardening*. Dallas, TX: Taylor Publishing.

Thomas, W. H. (1996). *Life worth living: The Eden Alternative in action*. Acton, MA: VanderWyk & Burnham.

Thomas, W. H. (1998). *Open hearts, open minds*. New York, NY: Summer Hill Co.

Wells, S. E. (Ed.). (1997). *Horticultural therapy and the older adult population*. New York, NY: The Haworth Press.

Yeomans, K. (1992) *The able gardener: Overcoming barriers of age and physical limitations*. Pownal, VT: Storey Books.

Gardening for Wildlife and Companion Animals

ASPCA National Animal Poison Control Center. (1998, July). *Household plant reference* (revised). Urbana, IL: Author. *Available from:* ASPCA/APCC Household Plant Reference, 1717 South Philo Road, Suite #36, Urbana, IL 61802. *Cost:* $15 (includes postage).

Backyard Wildlife Habitat Program
National Wildlife Federation
8925 Leesburg Pike, Vienna, VA 22184–0001
To become certified as a Backyard Wildlife Habitat, write for their certification packet.

Bourne, R. (Ed.). (1974). *Gardening with wildlife: The official backyard habitat planning and planting kit*. Washington, DC: Author.

Brooklyn Botanic Garden
1000 Washington Ave., Brooklyn, NY 11225

Center for Plant Conservation
Missouri Botanical Garden
PO Box 299, St. Louis, MO 63166

Cooperative Extension Service Offices are listed under county government in the phone book.

Frazier, A. with Eckroati, N. (1990). *The new natural cat: A complete guide for finicky owners.* New York, NY: E. P. Dutton.

Herr, J., Larson, Y., and Libbey, Y. (1997). *Creative resources: Birds and animals.* Albany, NY: Delmar Learning.

House Rabbit Society. (1994). *The facts about poinsettia.* Retrieved from: http://www.rabbit.org/care/poinsettia.html

Hylton, W. H. (Ed.) (1974). *The Rodale herb book: How to use, grow, and buy Nature's miracle plants.* Emmaus, PA: Rodale Press.

Kress, S. W. (Ed.) (1998). *Bird gardens.* Pownal, VT: Storey Books.

McGinnis, T. (1996). *The well cat book: The classic comprehensive handbook of cat care.* New York, NY: Random House.

National Audubon Society. (1977). *Guide to North American birds (Eastern region).* New York, NY: Alfred A. Knopf.

National Audubon Society. (1977). *Guide to North American birds (Western region).* New York, NY: Alfred A. Knopf.

Naturescape
P.O. Box 9354 Stn. Prov. Gov., Victoria, BC, Canada V8W 9M1

Proctor, N. (1986). *Garden birds.* Emmaus, PA: Rodale Press.

Sibley, D. A. (2000). *National Audubon Society guide to birds.* New York, NY: Alfred A Knopf.

State Department of Natural Resources, Division of Wildlife can be found in the phone book. Ask for information about **State Native Plant Societies**, wildlife, and other resources in your area.

Stein, D. (1993). *Natural healing for dogs and cats.* Freedom, CA: Crossing Press.

Stokes, D. and Stokes, L. (1991). *Stokes butterfly book: The complete guide to butterfly gardening, identification and behavior.* Boston, MA: Little, Brown and Co.

Wild Ones—Natural Landscapers, Ltd.
P.O. Box 23576, Milwaukee, WI 53223–0576
Provides a handbook with membership.

Yarnell, C. (1995). *Cat care, naturally: Celeste Yarnell's complete guide to holistic healthcare for cats.* Boston, MA: Charles C. Tuttle.

Gardening Supplies and Resources

Barton, B. J. (1997). *Gardening by mail: A source book.* (5th ed.). Boston, MA: Houghton Mifflin.

Logee's Greenhouses, Ltd.
141 North Street, Danielson, CT 06239–1939.
Phone: 888–330–8038; or 860–774–8038
Fax: 888–774–9932
Web site: http://www.logees.com
Specializes in Passion flower (Passaflora varieties) and other tropical and subtropical plants.

George W. Park Seed Company
1 Parkton Avenue, Greenwood, SC 29649
Toll free: 1–800–213–0076
Web site: http://www.parkseed.com
Annual, perennial, herb and vegetable seeds for American gardens. Also carries bulbs, fruits, supplies, equipment, and statuary for gardens.

Reilly, A. (1992). *Park's success with seeds.* New York, NY: Scribner.

The Bug Store
113 W. Argonne
St. Louis, MO 63122–1104
Toll-free: 1–800–455–2847
Send for their catalog of beneficial insects.

Thompson and Morgan, Ltd.
   P.O. Box 1308, Jackson, NJ 08527–0308
   Toll-free: 1–800–274–7333
   Offers online catalogs, gardening information. Seed catalog available.

Houseplant Care and Indoor Gardening

There are numerous resources for houseplant care. See the excellent list at the back of Life Worth Living *(Thomas, 1996).*

Halpern, A. M. (Ed.). (1980). *Rodale's encyclopedia of indoor gardening.* Emmaus, PA: Rodale Press.

Hylton, W. H. (Ed.) (1974). *The Rodale herb book: How to use, grow, and buy Nature's miracle plants.* Emmaus, PA: Rodale Press.

Kramer, J. (1999). *Easy-care guide to houseplants.* Upper Saddle River, NJ: Creative Homemaker Press.

Lancaster, R. and Biggs, M. (1998). *What houseplant where?* New York, NY: DK Publishing.

Thomas, W. H. (1996). *Life worth living: The Eden Alternative in action.* Acton, MA: VanderWyk & Burnham.

Wolverton, B. C. (1997). *How to grow fresh air: 50 houseplants that purify your home or office.* New York, NY: Penguin Books.

Intergenerational Activities and Working with Children

Local botanical gardens are also an excellent resource for ideas and activities for working with children.

Charner, K. (Ed.). (1997). *Everything for fall—A complete activity book for teachers of young children: Activities for September, October and November.* Beltsville, MD: Gryphon House.

Children's gardening resource directory. Available from: Cleveland Botanical Garden, 11030 East Boulevard, Cleveland, OH, 44106.

Phone: 216–721–1600. Also their Hershey Children's Garden at the same location. Retrieved from http://www.cbgarden.org

Gryphon House. (2002). Retrieved from: http://www.ghbooks.com Site contains many free nature and gardening activity resources for children.

Herd, M. (1997). *Learn and play in the garden.* Haupauge, NY: Barron's Juveniles.

Herr, J., Larson, Y., and Libbey, Y. (1997). *Creative resources: Birds and animals.* Albany, NY: Delmar Learning.

Kerrigan, J. and Stevenson, N. C. (1997). Behavioral study of youth and elders in an intergenerational horticultural program. In S. E. Wells (Ed.), *Horticultural therapy and the older adult population.* Binghamton, NY: Haworth.

Kreidler, B. (2001). Gardening in mixed company: Laying the groundwork for elders and kids. *The Eden Alternative Journal, 9*(2), 12–13.

Lalli, V. A., Tennessen, D. J., and Lockhart, K. (1998). *Using plants to bridge the generations.* Ithaca, NY: Cornell Cooperative Extension.

Lovejoy, S. (1999). *Roots, shoots, buckets and boots: Gardening together with children.* New York, NY: Workman Publishing.

Ocone, L. (Ed.) (1990). *National Gardening Association guide to kids' gardening.* New York, NY: Wiley and Sons.

Ocone, L. and Pranis, E. (1983). *The youth gardening book: A complete guide for teachers, parents and youth leaders.* Burlington, VT: Gardens for All.

Roots and shoots: Intergenerational gardening curriculum guide. Available from: The Elizabeth F. Gamble Garden Center, 1431 Waverly Street, Palo Alto, CA 94301. *Phone:* 650–329–1356. Retrieved from: http://www.gamblegarden.org/garden/grdnrts.html

Sirett, D. and Tankel. L. (1997). *Play and learn: Growing things.* New York, NY: DK Publishing.

Walczek, T. (rev. by S. Lineberger) (1998). KinderGARDEN: A web page. College

Station, TX: Dept of Horticultural Sciences, Texas A&M University. Retrieved from: http://aggie-horticulture.tamu.edu/kindergarden/kinder.htm

Read-to-Me Books

Crebbin, J. (1995). *Danny's duck*. Cambridge, MA: Candlewick Press.

Herriot, J. (1993). *The Christmas day kitten*. New York, NY: St. Martin's Press.

Loewer, P. and Loewer, J. (1998). *The moonflower*. Atlanta, GA: Peachtree Press.

Maass, R. (1996). *When spring comes*. New York, NY: Henry Holt and Co.

McNulty, F. (1994). *A snake in the house*. New York, NY: Scholastic Inc.

Reed-Jones, C. (1995). *The tree in the ancient forest*. Nevada City, CA: Dawn Publications.

Ryder, J. (1999). *Snail's spell*. New York, NY: Econo-Clad Books.

Sanders, S. R. (1998). *Warm as wool*. Aladdin Paperbacks.

Sharp, A. (1995). *The koala book*. Gretna, LA: Pelican Publishing.

Slepian, J. (1995). *Lost moose*. New York, NY: Philomel Books.

Stewart, S. (1997). *The gardener*. New York, NY: Farrar, Straus, Giroux.

Song

Mallett, D. (1997). Inch-by-inch: The garden song. In J. Denver (2001), *John Denver anthology* (rev. ed.). Port Charles, NY: Cherry Lane Books.

Miscellaneous

Harris' farmer's almanac. New York, NY: Harris Publications.

James, T. (1990). *The potpourri gardener*. New York, NY: Hungry Minds.

Old farmer's almanac. Dublin, NH: Yankee Publishing, Inc.

Reader's Digest Editors. (1981). *Back to basics*. New York, NY: Putnam Group.

Riotte, L. (1987). *Sleeping with a sunflower: A treasury of old-time gardening lore*. Pownal, VT: Storey Books.

Wegerzyn Horticultural Center. (February 1999). Handbook from seminar: *At home with native plants: Creating residential habitats*. Dayton, OH: Author.

Flower Activities

Bailey, L. (1997). *Country flowers: Gardening bouquets from spring to fall*. New York, NY: Random House.

Condon, G. (1982). *The complete book of flower preservation*. Englewood Cliffs, NJ: Prentice-Hall.

Jenkins, E. (1993). *Pleasure of the garden*. New York, NY: Crown.

Pertuit, A. J. (2002). *Drying flowers*. Clemson University's Extension Fact Sheet. Retrieved from http://hgic.clemson.edu/factsheets/HGIC1151.htm

Rothenberger, R. R. (2000). *Drying flowers and foliage for arrangements*. Ag. Pub. G6540. Columbia, MO: University of Missouri, Columbia. Retrieved from http://muextension.missouri.edu/xplor/agguides/hort/g06540.htm

Wood, E. and Merer, J. (1985). *Flowercrafts: Decorating and designing with flowers and floral motifs*. New York, NY: HarperCollins.

Organic Gardening Practices

Investigate Internet web sites at university agricultural departments. Use keywords such as organic gardening, companion planting, biological controls. Ask an Internet savvy staff member, resident, or volunteer to help search for specific information. Be prepared with a detailed list of subjects, organizations, and names. Many useful descriptions, photos, and lists from the Internet can be printed and kept in a reference notebook.

Bradley, F. M. and Ellis, B. W. (Eds.). (1992). *Rodale's all-new encyclopedia of organic gardening: The indispensible resource for every gardener*. Emmaus, PA: Rodale Press.

Denckla, T. (1994). *The organic gardener's home reference: A plant-by-plant guide to growing fresh, healthy food*. Williamstown, MA: Storey Publications.

Hillers, V. (1998). Guidelines for Using Manure on Vegetable Gardens. *Foodsafety Resource Page,* Washington State University. Retrieved from http://foodsafety.wsu.edu/factsheet/asp?pid=83

Jones, G. M. (2000, May). Animal Manure May Contain Disease-Causing Bacteria, Viruses That Can Reduce Water Quality. *Dairy Pipeline*. Blacksburg, VA: Virginia Cooperative Extension. Retrieved from http://www.ext.vt.edu/news/periodicals/dairy/2000-05/manure.html

Long, C. and McGrath, M. (1994, Jul/Aug). Treated Wood. *Organic Gardening Magazine, 41*(1), 71–74.
A complete bibliography of scientific studies is available for $2 by writing to OG Treated Wood Woes, 33 E. Minor Street, Emmaus, PA 18098.

Organic Trade Association. *Manure use and agricultural practices*. Fact sheet retrieved from http://www.ota.com/facts_manure.htm

Riotte, L. (1998). *Carrots love tomatoes: Secrets of companion planting for successful gardening* (rev. ed.). Pownal, VT: Storey Books.

Yepsin, R. B., Jr. (1984). *The encyclopedia of natural insect and disease control*. Emmaus, PA: Rodale Press.

Outdoor Gardening

Bailey, L. (1997). *Lee Bailey's country flowers: Gardening boquets from spring to fall*. New York, NY: Random House.

Bradley, S. and Berry, S. (2000). *The practical guide to container gardening*. Williamstown, MA: Storey Publications.

Brennan, G. (1998). *Backyard bouquets*. San Francisco, CA: Chronicle Books.

Cox, F. (1995). *Seasons in a country garden*. Golden, CO: Fulcrum Publishing.

Creasy, R. (1982). *The complete book of edible landscaping*. San Francisco, CA: Sierra Club Books.

Creasy, R. (2000). *The edible flower garden*. Boston, MA: Periplus Editions.

Felton, E. (1990). *Artistically cultivated herbs: How to train herbs as a decorative art*. Santa Barbara, CA: Woodbridge Press.

Hylton, W. H. (Ed.). (1974). *The Rodale herb book: How to use, grow, and buy Nature's miracle plants*. Emmaus, PA: Rodale Press.

Kress, S. W. (Ed.). (1998). *Bird gardens*. Pownal, VT: Storey Books.

Lewis, A. (1995). *Butterfly gardens: Luring Nature's lovliest pollinators to your yard*. New York, NY: Brooklyn Botanic Garden.

Powell, E. (1995). *From seed to bloom: How to grow over 500 annuals, perennials and herbs* (rev. ed.). Pownal, VT: Storey Books.

Raven, S. (1996). *The cutting garden: Growing and arranging garden flowers*. New York, NY: Reader's Digest Adult.

Reppert, B. (1996). *Growing and using rosemary*. Pownal, VT: Storey Publications.

Reilly, A. (1992). *Park's success with seeds*. New York, NY: Scribner.

Schmidt, J. C. (2002). *Growing herbs in the home garden*. Publ VC-44-93. Champaign, IL: University of Illinois, Dept. of Horticulture. Retrieved from: http://www.aces.uiuc.edu/NRES/extension/factsheets/vc-44/VC-44.html

Schmidt, J. C. and Noland, D. (2002). *Harvesting and drying herbs*. Publ. NRES-VC 31-97. Champaign, IL: University of Illinois, Dept. of Horticulture. Retrieved from: http://www.ag.uiuc.edu/~vista/pdf_pubs/DRYHERBS.pdf

Schultz, W. (1997). *For your garden: Vines and climbers*. New York, NY: Friedman/Fairfax.

Simmons, A. G. (1992). *Herb gardening in five seasons: An illustrated guide to cultivating herbs for recipes, decorations and gifts.* New York, NY: E. P. Dutton.

Toxic Plant Information and Plant Identification

Check with your local poison control center for various fliers about and lists of toxic plants in your region.

ASPCA National Animal Poison Control Center. (1998, July). *Household plant reference* (revised). Urbana, IL: Author. *Available from:* ASPCA/APCC Household Plant Reference, 1717 South Philo Road, Suite #36, Urbana, IL 61802. *Cost:* $15 (includes postage).

Burrows, G. E. and Tyrl, R. J. (2001). *Toxic plants of North America.* Ames, IA: Iowa State University Press.

Greater Cleveland Poison Control Center, 11100 Euclid Avenue, Cleveland, OH 44106–6010. *Phone:* 216–844–1573 (administrative office). *Offers various fliers and lists of toxic plants.*

Halpin, A. M. (Ed.) (1980). *Rodale's encyclopedia of indoor gardening.* Emmaus, PA: Rodale Press.

House Rabbit Society. (1994). *The facts about poinsettia.* Retrieved from: http://www.rabbit.org/care/poinsettia.html

King, A. I. (2002). *Toxic plants.* University of California Davis Cooperative Extension. Retrieved from http://envhort.ucdavis.edu/ce/king/PoisPlant/Tox-com.htm

Master Gardeners of Hancock County Ohio. (2002). *Children are berry curious: A guide to the hazards of ingestion of raw berries in northwest Ohio.* Retrieved from: http://hancock.osu.edu/hort/berrybook.pdf

Monro, D. B. (2002). Canadian Poisonous Plants Information System, Agriculture and Agri-Food Canada. Retrieved from http://sis.agr.gc.ca/pls/pp/poison?p_x=px

Thieret, J. W., Niering, W. A., and Olmstead, N. C. (2001). *The Audubon society field guide to North American wildflowers, Eastern region.* New York, NY: Alfred A. Knopf.

Turner, R. J. and Wasson, E. (Eds.). (1997). *Botanica.* Sydney: Random House Australia.

UC Regents. (1998). *Toxicity of Plants.* Safety Information/Wellness, University of California at Davis. Retrieved from http://wellness.ucdavis.edu/safety_info/poison_prevention/take_care_with_plants/toxicity_of_plants.html

Appendix
Fill-in Forms

Indoor Plant Donation Request

The residents of _____ are very happy to accept your gifts of live plants and blooming flowers to enhance our resident areas. Please make your selection(s) from the list below and obtain a **Donor Form**. To prevent duplications, please notify a staff member of your choices prior to purchase. We have the following requests for this living area:

Unit Name: _____

Location for Plants: _____

Exposure: _____

Our Plant Choices

TYPE OF PLANT	POT SIZE	NUMBER WANTED

Additional Needs:

NOTE TO DONORS:

Please include a label for each plant with its common and botanical name if possible. The plants should be kept in the pots in which they were purchased. If saucers are not attached, please include a clear plastic saucer one size larger than the pot. Thank you.

If you have any questions, please call: _____

Indoor Plant Donor Form

The residents of _____ are very happy to accept your gifts of live plants and flowers to enhance our resident areas. **Please CIRCLE your selection(s) from the list below. To prevent duplications, please notify a staff member of your choices prior to purchase. We have requests for the following living area:**

Unit Name: _____

Location for Plants: _____

Exposure: _____

PLANT CHOICES

TYPE OF PLANT	POT SIZE	NUMBER WANTED

Additional Needs:

NOTE TO DONORS:

Please include a **label with the common and botanical name for each plant** if possible. The plants should be kept in the pots in which they were purchased. If saucers are not attached, please include a clear plastic saucer one size larger than the pot. Thank you.

Please return this form with the plant(s) or any monetary donation.

NAME OF DONOR: _____

ADDRESS: _____

_____

If you have any questions, please call: _____

WEEKLY INDOOR PLANT CARE NOTES

LOCATION: _____

PLANTS: _____

_____

_____

_____

DATE & PERSON	ROUTINE CARE	FERTILIZED	COMMENTS

Index

Other Books by Venture Publishing, Inc.

Leisure Education Program Planning: A Systematic Approach, Second Edition
by John Dattilo

Leisure Education Specific Programs
by John Dattilo

Leisure in Your Life: An Exploration, Fifth Edition
by Geoffrey Godbey

Leisure Services in Canada: An Introduction, Second Edition
by Mark S. Searle and Russell E. Brayley

Leisure Studies: Prospects for the Twenty-First Century
edited by Edgar L. Jackson and Thomas L. Burton

The Lifestory Re-Play Circle: A Manual of Activities and Techniques
by Rosilyn Wilder

Models of Change in Municipal Parks and Recreation: A Book of Innovative Case Studies
edited by Mark E. Havitz

More Than a Game: A New Focus on Senior Activity Services
by Brenda Corbett

Nature and the Human Spirit: Toward an Expanded Land Management Ethic
edited by B. L. Driver, Daniel Dustin, Tony Baltic, Gary Elsner, and George Peterson

Outdoor Recreation Management: Theory and Application, Third Edition
by Alan Jubenville and Ben Twight

Planning Parks for People, Second Edition
by John Hultsman, Richard L. Cottrell, and Wendy Z. Hultsman

The Process of Recreation Programming Theory and Technique, Third Edition
by Patricia Farrell and Herberta M. Lundegren

Programming for Parks, Recreation, and Leisure Services: A Servant Leadership Approach
by Donald G. DeGraaf, Debra J. Jordan, and Kathy H. DeGraaf

Protocols for Recreation Therapy Programs
edited by Jill Kelland, along with the Recreation Therapy Staff at Alberta Hospital Edmonton

Quality Management: Applications for Therapeutic Recreation
edited by Bob Riley

A Recovery Workbook: The Road Back from Substance Abuse
by April K. Neal and Michael J. Taleff

Recreation and Leisure: Issues in an Era of Change, Third Edition
edited by Thomas Goodale and Peter A. Witt

Recreation Economic Decisions: Comparing Benefits and Costs, Second Edition
by John B. Loomis and Richard G. Walsh

Recreation for Older Adults: Individual and Group Activities
by Judith A. Elliott and Jerold E. Elliott

Recreation Programming and Activities for Older Adults
by Jerold E. Elliott and Judith A. Sorg-Elliott

Reference Manual for Writing Rehabilitation Therapy Treatment Plans
by Penny Hogberg and Mary Johnson

Research in Therapeutic Recreation: Concepts and Methods
edited by Marjorie J. Malkin and Christine Z. Howe

Simple Expressions: Creative and Therapeutic Arts for the Elderly in Long-Term Care Facilities
by Vicki Parsons

A Social History of Leisure Since 1600
by Gary Cross

A Social Psychology of Leisure
by Roger C. Mannell and Douglas A. Kleiber

Steps to Successful Programming: A Student Handbook to Accompany Programming for Parks, Recreation, and Leisure Services
by Donald G. DeGraaf, Debra J. Jordan, and Kathy H. DeGraaf

Stretch Your Mind and Body: Tai Chi as an Adaptive Activity
by Duane A. Crider and William R. Klinger

Therapeutic Activity Intervention with the Elderly: Foundations & Practices
by Barbara A. Hawkins, Marti E. May, and Nancy Brattain Rogers

Therapeutic Recreation and the Nature of Disabilites
by Kenneth E. Mobily and Richard MacNeil

Therapeutic Recreation: Cases and Exercises, Second Edition
by Barbara C. Wilhite and M. Jean Keller

Therapeutic Recreation in Health Promotion and Rehabilitation
by John Shank and Catherine Coyle

Therapeutic Recreation in the Nursing Home
by Linda Buettner and Shelley L. Martin

Therapeutic Recreation Protocol for Treatment of Substance Addictions
by Rozanne W. Faulkner

Tourism and Society: A Guide to Problems and Issues
by Robert W. Wyllie

A Training Manual for Americans with Disabilities Act Compliance in Parks and Recreation Settings
by Carol Stensrud

Venture Publishing, Inc.
1999 Cato Avenue
State College, PA 16801
phone: 814-234-4561
fax: 814-234-1651